What is Accounting

Other *What is . . .?* books available

Linguistics
Psychology
Communication Studies
Social Anthropology

in preparation

Engineering
Religious Studies
Business Studies

What is
Accounting?

Geoff Hardern

Assistant Director,
Trent Polytechnic

Edward Arnold

© Geoff Hardern 1985

First published in Great Britain 1985 by
Edward Arnold (Publishers) Ltd,
41 Bedford Square, London WC1B 3DQ

Edward Arnold (Australia) Pty Ltd,
80 Waverley Road, Caulfield East,
Victoria 3145, Australia

Edward Arnold, 300 North Charles Street,
Baltimore, Maryland 21201, USA

British Library Cataloguing in Publication Data

Hardern, Geoff
  What is accounting?
  1. Accounting
  I. Title
  657   HF5635

  ISBN 0-7131-6444-1

Text set in 10/11pt Times Compugraphic
by Colset Private Ltd, Singapore
Printed and bound by Richard Clay
(The Chaucer Press) Bungay, Suffolk.

Contents

vi *Contents*

Preface

This short book sets out to answer the question 'What is accounting' by considering in turn a number of separate but related questions: What are accounts and why are they kept? What is it that accountants actually do? How is accounting changing in the modern world? What are the aims and content of higher education courses in accounting? It is clearly impossible to give a full answer to all these questions in the space available. The intention is to give the 'flavour' of accounting practice relying heavily on analogies and illustrative examples rather than attempt an extensive survey of accounting techniques.

The book is primarily intended for young people who are either thinking seriously about a career in accountancy or who are about to start their accounting studies and wish to have an overview of the subject. The emphasis is on the nature of accounting as a practical activity and as an academic discipline. It is not intended as a complete guide to careers in accounting or a source of detailed information about the various routes towards professional qualification in the United Kingdom, although some general guidance on these matters is included in the appendices.

As careful readers of the above paragraph may have detected, there is some semantic confusion between the words 'accounting' and 'accountancy'. Dictionaries usually define 'accountancy' as the profession of the accountant or the general principles which guide this activity and 'accounting' as the skills and techniques used in practice. However, the words are often used interchangeably with a growing tendency to prefer the term 'accounting' – a practice which is followed in this book.

In the modern world, much economic activity is carried out by large complex organizations and the accounts must reflect this complexity if they are to give a true and fair picture of economic realities. A basic accounting textbook can easily give an air of unreality to the subject by introducing the reader to the accounts of simple fictitious organizations such as 'John Smith and Co. Ltd'. The advantages of using a practical case study of accounting in action seem to outweigh the dangers of introducing the reader to unnecessary accounting technicalities. Chapter 2 on business accounting is therefore based on the published accounts of an actual public limited company.

I am grateful to the finance director of the Burton Group plc for permission to quote extracts from the company's 1983 annual report and accounts. Professor Pierre Seneque of the University of Natal, John Bull of Plymouth Polytechnic and Fred Langley of Leeds Polytechnic have saved me from some of the many traps that are set for those who attempt to simplify such a complex subject. Any remaining errors, omissions and distortions are my responsibility. My publishers have given me much helpful advice on presentation, and Mrs Sue Marshall has coped with a difficult, near illegible manuscript with her customary efficiency; my sincere thanks to them all.

1
What is Accounting?

I received (less agent's commissions) about £16,000 during the year, which may be called success by any worldly-minded author. It is apparently as much as I had earned during all the previous part of my life. And I bought a car and yacht and arranged to buy a house.

> Arnold Bennett, *Journals*, entry for 31 December 1912

A merchant settles his accounts for the year *c*.1390:

> And up into his counting house goeth he
> To reckon with himself [en], well may be.
> Of that same year how that it with him stood,
> And how that he dispended had his good
> And if that he increased were or no.

> Chaucer, *The Canterbury Tales: The Shipman's Tale*
> (spelling modernized)

What are accounts?

It is the Annual General Meeting of the local football club. The next item on the agenda is the presentation of the annual accounts by the club Treasurer. 'I am sure that you have all read the Income and Expenditure account and Balance Sheet which were sent out with the papers for the meeting. They have been agreed by the auditor, of course. As you can see, we made a small surplus last year and the bank balance is reasonably healthy. I think the accounts are self-explanatory and I do not propose to go through them in detail but I will be happy to answer any questions.' There is a slight pause as the members quickly glance through their papers. The Treasurer answers a

1

question about travelling expenses and reassures another member that there is no need to increase the subscription. The accounts are adopted, the Chairman thanks the Treasurer and the meeting quickly moves on to the next item of business.

The presentation of accounts at the annual general meetings of organizations ranging from small sports clubs to large public limited companies often seems like a formal ritual, giving members a vague general assurance that their finances are not being mismanaged. Everyone agrees that regular accounting reports are necessary and that they should be properly prepared and presented but what do they really mean? Should all the figures be treated as hard, indisputable facts or does the form and content of an accounting report depend to a large extent on the skill and judgement of the accountant? Do the accounts help us to assess the financial health (whatever that means) of the organization? Will the accounts help managers to make better decisions? These questions emphasize the link between sound accounting practice and the successful management of business enterprises and non-profit making organizations alike.

However, the principles of sound financial management have an even wider application and are relevant for any type of economic activity. The private citizen in his capacity of 'economic man' may keep personal accounts. Local authorities must prepare accounts to show how receipts from ratepayers and central government are spent on such services as education, police and social services. At the level of the national economy, the success or failure of government economic policies is heavily dependent on the accuracy of national income accounts. These accounts attempt to measure the main flows in the economy between broad sectors such as business, central government and households, subdivided into such elements as total personal saving, corporate taxation or the capital investment of nationalized industries.

The value of sound accounting practice may be illustrated by looking at the financial affairs of the private individual. Apart from their relative simplicity, there are other advantages in starting with personal accounts rather than, say, the accounts of a large limited company (a subject reserved for Chapter 2). A study of personal accounts shows that I need not be a professional accountant to apply the principles of accounting to my own finances; everyone can be his or her own accountant, provided the taxation problems are not too difficult! There is no doubt that most of us would benefit from paying more attention to the way in which we manage our finances. We may keep some account of our financial transactions, if only on the back of an envelope or scribbled on the bank statement. Home computer salesmen are always ready to help us install our own personal accounting system if we need a more detailed analysis.

Let us assume that I have the time, energy and inclination to draft a complete personal accounting system. What sort of information do I need and how will it help me to manage my affairs? There are at least six separate answers to this question and, by examining each in turn, we can learn a great deal about accounting theory and practice. Why, then, should I keep personal accounts?

Six reasons for keeping personal accounts

1 To make sure I am living within my income My main source of income is a salary, paid monthly, supplemented by interest on a building society account and dividends from a small unit trust holding. I seem to have no difficulty in spending this income. Income tax and National Insurance contributions are deducted from my gross monthly salary by my employer. Much of my net income goes on items such as food and drink, clothing, travel costs, heating, lighting, rates and insurance, which I regard as basic necessities. The remainder is 'discretionary' expenditure on entertainment, holidays, books, periodicals, records and the like.

I have decided to record all these items in an income and expenditure account to show whether I have made a surplus or a deficit over the year. The surplus or deficit on this account will tell me whether I am living beyond my income or not. Mr Micawber, in *Great Expectations* by Charles Dickens, recognized the importance of income and expenditure accounting even if he did little about it in practice:

Annual income twenty pounds, annual expenditure nineteen nineteen six, result happiness. Annual income twenty pounds, annual expenditure twenty pounds ought and six, result misery.

In preparing my income and expenditure statement I must remember to draw a distinction between items of current expenditure and the ways in which I use the current surplus in the form of gifts or saving. In particular I must exclude regular contractual savings such as premiums on an endowment insurance policy and 'compulsory' saving such as contributions to a superannuation scheme. I shall reap the benefits from these payments in the future (provided I live to see it) when the insurance policy matures and when I draw my pension.

Payments for major capital items of lasting value are also excluded. When I buy a car I shall expect to derive benefit from its use over a number of years. The total capital cost of the car will be spread over the years and not shown as a single cost in the year of purchase. Mortgage repayments are also a problem (in more ways than one). My monthly repayments include an element of capital repayment and an interest charge on the total loan outstanding. I should only charge the interest element as a current expense. The capital repayment is helping to build up my net assets (an owner-occupied house) and should be excluded from the income and expenditure account.

Finally I must be careful to make a distinction between income and expenditure relating to a period of time and actual cash receipts and payments over the same period of time. The two are not necessarily the same. My rates demand from the local council is in respect of the financial year which runs from April to March. It is payable in two equal instalments and by 31 December I have settled in full for the whole financial year. When I come to make up my accounts on 31 December I must make an adjustment in the income and expenditure account to allow for the unexpired portion of the rates paid. Adjustments must also be made for expenses which have accrued but have not yet been paid at year end; although I have still not paid a bill to the plumber for work which he did in October, the cost of the work must be charged to the income and expenditure account for the year.

2 To find out what I am worth   Let us assume that I live in a detached house (freehold) in the suburbs, full of modern furniture and various household gadgets. I drive a Ford Sierra car which I am paying for myself; (I do not have the benefit of a company car). On 31 December I have a bank balance of £150 and £50 in cash. The balance of my building society account is £800 and my unit trust holding is worth £2,500. My neighbour, Mr Jones, who has been trying to keep up with me (or is it the other way round?) lives in the same type of house, owns the same model of car and has an identical list of other assets.

I have decided to follow Arnold Bennett's example and take stock of my affairs at the end of the calendar year. Accordingly, I draw up a balance sheet to show the position at 31 December. I list the values of all my assets and then deduct any liabilities, or amounts owed by me on 31 December to show the total value of my net assets. Mr Jones carries out the same exercise. Asset values are the same for us both but unfortunately, although Mr Jones has no liabilities at the year end, I have an outstanding HP commitment of £1,000 on the car, a mortgage liability of £5,000 and various unpaid bills amounting to £280. When all the calculations are complete, it appears from the balance sheets that my net assets are valued at a figure which is £6,280 less than the valuation of Mr Jones's net worth, the difference being the extent of my liabilities.

We can learn much about balance sheet construction from this simple example. Balance sheets record *net* worth or total assets less total liabilities. There are two broad groups of assets: current assets, such as cash in hand and my bank balance which changes from day to day, and fixed assets such as my house and car. A balance sheet gives a snapshot view of the position at a particular point in time, whereas an income and expenditure account records incoming and outgoing flows relating to a period of time.

It might be thought that assets should always be shown in my balance sheet at cost: if I have just paid £750 for a new hi-fi system, that presumably is what it is worth to me. Unfortunately, asset valuation is not as simple as this. Let us assume that I bought my house several years ago for £8,500 before the boom in house prices, and the local estate agent currently values it at £45,000. In this case I would be grossly understating the value of the house if I were to include it in my balance sheet at cost.

If the house has appreciated in value, my car has lost £2,000 in value if I compare its current trade-in value (£5,000) with what I paid for it a year ago (£7,000). A motor car is a depreciating asset. How should I value my furniture? As most of it was bought several years ago, an historical cost valuation would not be particularly helpful. Apart from antique items, furniture deteriorates over time so perhaps I should reduce the cost value of each item by a depreciation allowance to represent the wear and tear suffered. Alternatively I might decide to list each item of furniture at its current value. However, the idea of 'current value' is open to at least two possible interpretations. Does it mean the amount that I would receive if I were to sell it as second hand furniture? – not very much in practice. On the other hand, does 'current value' mean the cost of replacing all the items of furniture if they were destroyed by fire tomorrow? – a much larger sum. A discussion of all these issues would soon take us into the realm of accounting theory.

Apart from a desire to satisfy my natural curiosity about what I am currently worth, is there any practical need to prepare a personal balance sheet? Unfortunately most of the reasons for making formal valuations of personal assets and liabilities tend to be associated with the more gloomy aspects of life. The need to insure my house and its contents against fire and other risks at a full valuation is an obvious example. Statements of affairs in bankruptcy are another. In our simple example, total assets were greater than total liabilities. Let us now assume that, as a result of a series of rash speculations on the stock market, I have incurred massive debts in excess of my total assets; in other words my net worth is negative. I am advised that the only way out is to be declared bankrupt and arrange for such assets as can be realized to be shared between my creditors as the law determines. A statement of affairs will be drawn up to account for the position. Finally (in two senses) my estate will need to be valued on my death to determine any liability for capital transfer tax and to enable my executors to carry out my wishes. They will settle any outstanding debts and distribute the remaining surplus in accordance with my Will.

There is another side to the construction of balance sheets apart from the valuation of net assets; we must also determine their *ownership*. We have seen that total assets less any liabilities or obligations to outsiders is equivalent to net worth or *capital*. Throughout the previous discussion I have assumed, with characteristic egotism, that this value represents my personal ownership of the net assets. Of course my wife might have some strong views on this matter as our household assets have been built up over the years as a joint effort. The divorce courts are daily having to share out matrimonial property on the breakdown of marriages. The point is that any balance sheet must refer to a defined 'entity' or distinct area of economic activity and questions of ownership must be answered in relation to that entity. In this case the entity is best defined as a household: this is certainly the view taken by the Inland Revenue for income tax purposes unless husband and wife ask to be separately assessed. Provided the marriage is a going concern, there is fortunately no need to be precise about the respective shares of husband and wife in the ownership of the net assets of the household. In the case of a business partnership, however, it would be essential to show clearly how much each partner had contributed and what each share is now worth.

3 To make sure I can meet my commitments Although my income and expenditure account shows that I am living within my income over the year as a whole, I might still face an awkward cash flow problem if, for instance, I have to meet the cost of the Christmas festivities and know that I will be out of funds until my next salary cheque is paid into the bank on 21 January. I receive my salary in regular, fairly equal amounts each month. Outgoings tend to be more erratic, particularly when I have to meet large bills like the half year's rates or the cost of a major overhaul to the car. A cash budget would show me the likely pattern of cash receipts and payments over a period so that I could anticipate any shortfalls and arrange overdraft facilities with the bank. It is a valuable help in short term financial management.

The dangers of running short of cash are obvious; holding too much cash is also a mistake, even if the consequences are less dramatic. It is not in my best interest to keep a large permanent balance in my bank current account. I would be advised to transfer any excess over a reasonable working balance to a bank deposit account, a building society account or a similar form of investment. The money would then earn interest and yet still be reasonably accessible in case of need. Short term financial management helps me to make the best use of any idle cash balances as well as helping me to plan for any cash shortages.

4 To plan for the future   In addition to short term planning, I must look towards the future. I have decided that it is time to increase the provision for my old age. Accordingly I arrange to increase my holding of unit trusts by a regular payment of £50 per month through a standing order. As we have seen, such payments are not current expenditure and they should not appear in my income and expenditure account; the effect is rather to increase the value of one of my assets (investments). In the same way the cost of building an extension to the house is a capital payment of lasting value and would also increase the value of another of my assets (freehold property) and hence my net worth as shown in the balance sheet.

The decision to plan for the future does not only raise questions of how to record the transactions in my accounts. I may be able to meet some of my long term plans from regular saving from income but in other cases I will require long term finance. My house purchase is financed by a mortgage with a building society and my car under a hire purchase agreement. As we have seen, a simple cash budget will help my short term financial planning. I also need to have a long range financial plan if I am to make use of the most attractive sources of finance, minimize interest payments and secure the best tax advantage. For instance, as I am able to obtain tax relief on the interest payments on my mortgage but not on my hire purchase agreement, it will pay me to so arrange my affairs that I raise as much of my finance as possible through the mortgage.

5 The need to manage my affairs efficiently   My income seems to vanish as if by magic and I have only the vaguest idea about where it is going. What I require is my own personal management accounting system. Perhaps I should use my home computer to analyse my outgoings more precisely into such headings as car expenses, heat and light, food and drink and entertainment, as a first step to controlling expenses and eliminating waste. Am I really spending so much on the car? Perhaps I ought to sell it and buy a more economical model. I seem to be spending 50 per cent more on books and periodicals compared with the same period last year. I know that prices have risen, but this is ridiculous! The Victorian middle classes knew the value of well-kept household accounts. The stand-ard reference book was Mrs Beeton's *Household Management* which gave advice to the mistress of the house on such matters as purchasing and servant control, but also set out a detailed method of household cost analysis to account for the last halfpenny. The Victorians would have loved home computers!

Control is achieved by comparing actual expenditure with some yardstick in order to take effective corrective action. We have already hinted at one possible yardstick. This year's expenditure may be set against the equivalent period last year to indicate a trend, although the comparison may be mislead-ing if, for instance, there were exceptional items of expendi-ture last year. Budgets are a more effective basis for planning and control. I might set a target for each major group of expenses based on past experience and likely future develop-ments. My car expenses budget, for instance, will take account of the fact that I will need a new set of tyres next year. The separate expense budgets will be totalled and compared with my budgeted income to show my planned surplus for the year. I am now in a position to achieve a measure of control by comparing actual income and expenditure with these predeter-mined budgets. Any deviation or variance from the budget means that I should take some corrective action. If, by the third month of the year, I have already spent half of my enter-tainment budget, I must either cut down on this or some other head of expenditure for the remainder of the year.

6 To help me make sensible financial decisions I wish to replace my old television set; is it better to buy a new one outright or to rent one? I have the choice of travelling to work by car or taking the train. Which course of action would be the most economical? Before I reach these decisions I need some information about the relative costs of alternative courses of action. Only costs which are strictly relevant to the actual decision to be taken should be included in the comparison and I will have to go beyond the cost of past events as shown in my accounts and investigate likely future trends.

Let us take the decision about travelling to work as an exam-ple. I can divide the cost of running my car into two main groups. Car tax, insurance, garaging costs, my AA subscription, part of the depreciation in value over the year and an allowance for the interest on the money tied up in my 'investment' are all *fixed* annual costs which will be incurred whether I use the car for travelling to work or keep it locked in the garage. Petrol, oil, servicing costs, repairs, replacements and that part of depreciation which reflects wear and tear are *variable* costs which are related to the mileage on the clock. A moment's thought will show that when reaching my decision about travelling to work I should compare the rail fare with the variable car costs only. At present the cheap day rail return fare is £1.30. I estimate that my variable car costs are £1.91 per day (10.6p per mile for an 18 mile return journey). Other things being equal, I would be well advised to go to work by train.

This incursion into personal accounts has raised a number of general principles which must now be set into a wider context. In the next chapter we shall be looking in more detail at business accounting to show that the accounting needs of a large public limited company are no different in principle from the six reasons for keeping personal accounts which we have just identified. In one respect, however, there is a crucial difference between personal accounting and accounting for business, government agencies and other organizations. My personal accounts are only of interest to me (and possibly my tax inspector). The accounts of complex organizations such as large business corporations are of potential interest to a wide range of parties with different information needs. Internal management accounts will be prepared to help managers control costs and make sensible decisions. Public limited companies must publish financial accounts which are primarily intended for the benefit of shareholders, but also help to meet the information requirements of employees, creditors and providers of loan finance. Apart from these stakeholders who have a direct interest in the affairs of the company, it is clearly in the public interest that many other individuals, groups and organizations should have enough information to be able to make informed judgements about the company. The Inland Revenue's assessment of tax liability must be based on properly audited accounts. Economists, investment analysts and financial journalists all use the information contained in published company accounts. Potential investors need a clear indication of the past performance of the company and an honest indication of future prospects. Finally, the Government, opposition parties and indeed the public at large, are interested in monitoring the performance of the private business sector.

Accounting analogies: mirrors, maps and language

We can learn much about accounting by examining some simple analogies commonly used by accountants when talking about their subject. For instance, it is sometimes said that accounts should 'reflect' economic realities; Hamlet's advice to the players was that they should 'hold, as 'twere the mirror up to nature'. Is the role of the accountant to hold the mirror up to economic life? When reading figures in the published accounts of a large manufacturing company, we should be able to imagine the myriad transactions which lie behind the figures and visualize the plant, equipment, motor vehicles, cash, stock, and so on, represented by the various asset accounts. However, this ability of an accounting report to encapsulate a mass of data into a single figure shows the weakness of the mirror analogy. The accountant has an active role in the accounting process. Data is processed and condensed in accordance with certain conventions before being presented to the user.

The map is a better analogy than the mirror. A mapmaker represents the physical reality of the territory by using a number of standard conventions which should be well understood by users of the map. In case of doubt the conventional signs for different classes of roads, canals, churches with or without spires, and so on, are shown in a key. The preparation of the map has been preceded by a detailed survey to measure distances and heights above sea level. All this quantitative information is processed and presented on the map using such generally recognized conventions as drawing to scale and contour lines. By studying the contour lines, the map user will be able to make a reasonable judgement about the nature of the terrain. If he is a walker, for instance, he will know whether he is in for a hard, uphill slog or a pleasant stroll across undulating countryside.

Maps will be drawn to different scales to meet the needs of

different groups of map users. A world atlas will meet the needs of members of the general public who may wish to 'look up' countries, regions or cities mentioned in the news. At the other extreme, large-scale maps will be needed by town planners making decisions about changes in the use of land in a city. Economic, geological or historical maps would be prepared to meet the needs of specialist users. The choice of detail to be included in a map will also depend on user need. A road atlas for the motorist will not show contours, but will probably indicate mileage between towns. Physical or geological maps will not show administrative boundaries because unnecessary detail will obscure the main purpose of the map. If I do not find the precise information I require from a map, I will look at a different type of map, probably one drawn to a larger scale.

Accounting may be understood as a form of economic or financial mapmaking. The crew in Lewis Carroll's *Hunting of the Snark* understood the significance of conventions in mapmaking.

> 'What's the good of Mercator's North Poles and Equators, Tropics, Zones and Meridian Lines?'
> So the Bellman would cry: and the crew would reply
> 'They are merely conventional signs!'

Accountants, like cartographers, adopt conventional procedures for representing economic reality. At the most basic level similar types of transactions are grouped together into separate accounts using generally accepted account classifications such as sales, purchases, wages, etc. Details of each transaction are recorded separately and a balance is struck at the end of the accounting period or possibly after each transaction to show the net position of the account.

More fundamentally, accountants follow generally recognized conventions when approaching the task of recording economic events or valuing assets. In business accounting, for instance, it is always assumed that profit is realized when (and only when) a sale actually takes place. This is the accounting equivalent of the proverb 'Don't count your chickens before they are hatched'. This convention is just one example of the wider principle of conservatism or prudence which governs all aspects of accounting practice. The accountant's caution acts as a restraining influence on the salesman's optimism and modifies the businessman's rosy view of the company's future prospects. The analogy between maps and accounts may be taken further. Accounting 'maps' can be drawn to any scale from national income accounts to personal accounts, depending on the level of economic activity under consideration. Management accounts and published financial accounts emphasize different types of information because they are designed to meet the needs of different users. The accounts of a local authority are presented in a different format from the accounts of a public limited company. The reader may wish to test the analogy with reference to the American Accounting Association's definition of accounting as 'the process of identifying, measuring and communicating economic information to permit informed judgements and decisions by users of the information'. By substituting 'physical information' for 'economic information', the definition could easily be made to fit our criteria for successful mapmaking.

A close examination of the American Accounting Association's definition will disclose another possible analogy for accounting, probably more powerful than either the map or mirror analogies. According to that definition, accounting is a three-stage process. Data must be *identified* – the equivalent $c i$ 'first catch your hare' in the apocryphal recipe. Skills of *measurement* are important because accounts are kept in quantitative, usually financial, form. However, the final, and arguably the most important, stage of the process is one of *communication*. The accountant is a communicator; accounting reports will have limited value unless they are presented in ways which are intelligible and useful to users of the information. Accounting is therefore a form of *language;* the language of economic activity.

We shall try to develop this concept of accounting as a language in a number of directions, even if this strains the analogy to the limit. At first sight it might appear that the language of accounting is closely related to artificial computing languages such as BASIC or COBOL. An accounting text book setting out the generally accepted procedures, conventions and practices of accounting might be seen as equivalent to the manual of a high-level computing language. However, we must draw an important distinction between the two cases. A computing language is complete in itself; all its rules and vocabulary are contained in the manual. Unlike a natural language such as English, COBOL does not develop spontaneously in use. If I wish to write a program in a higher level of COBOL, for instance, I must use a new manual with a different, self-contained set of instructions.

It follows that accounting is best understood by analogy with a natural language such as English. An accounting text book is less like the manual of a computer language than a grammar text book or a guide to English usage. In the real world, businesses do not always keep their books in the 'correct' form as recommended in the standard text books, any more than we all use 'correct'. English as defined by a grammarian.

In fact, the accounting procedures to be found in the text books are simply a summary of what is currently considered to be good accounting practice and opinions about what is good accounting practice will change with time. As we all know, natural languages also change in spite of the determined attempts of such authoritative bodies as the Académie Française, founded in 1635 to purify and standardize the French language. Accounting practices are also subject to almost imperceptible changes over the years. The computerized accounts of a large multi-national company look very different from the accounts of an Elizabethan wool merchant, even if they are both recognizably written in the same language of accounting.

The language analogy can be taken a stage further. Although language is universal in all human societies, many separate languages are spoken throughout the world. In the same way, accounting practices are not universal; accounting systems in use in a country need to be understood in the context of the dominant social, political and economic system. For instance, in a planned economy such as the Soviet Union, the basic function of an accountant in an enterprise such as a steel works is to record the production costs of the enterprise as a basis for comparison with targets contained in a previously determined central plan. Methods for recording and classifying the relevant data will be laid down in detail by the state agency responsible for steel production. Accounting practice is therefore little more than routine book-keeping in accordance with standard procedures. The goal of the enterprise is usually to achieve certain production targets rather than make a return on capital employed, although in certain communist countries, notably Hungary, the concept of 'profit' is gaining ground in accounting practice.

In the capitalist world, the most significant developments in accounting techniques and practice have understandably been in the context of business accounting. In a pure capitalist system initiatives in economic affairs are left to private individuals and organizations operating in free markets. The State does not take a direct part in economic activities: its main role is to secure fair play in the market and so will try to make sure that information made available through published accounts is honest, reliable and meaningful. The efficient working of a market economy depends on an adequate flow of information and so accounting techniques should develop freely to meet the needs of the business community. Publicly available accounting information which is both 'true and fair' is essential, particulary in the working of capital markets where investors need to know whether a particular company is profitable, has sufficient reserves and has further growth potential. It is therefore inevitable that debates about accounting practice in capitalist countries centre round such issues as the measurement of profit, the valuation of assets and accounting for inflation which have a direct influence on the reporting of profits in the published accounts.

Of course, in the real world the State takes a more active role in economic affairs than might be suggested in this pure capitalist model. In such mixed economies as the United Kingdom, the growth of direct State activity has increased the significance of public service accounting. Nationalized industries in the UK are not run directly by government departments but by separate public corporations, such as the National Coal Board or the Gas Board. These boards have usually to meet social as well as commercial criteria and these responsibilities need to be reflected in the accounts. For instance, under the Railways Act 1974, the British Railways Board receives a grant for providing unremunerative passenger services (£933.4m in 1983). This compensation for carrying out its social obligation is added to the Board's commercial turnover to give a total turnover for the rail businesses of £2,925m.

The accounting needs of less developed countries (LDCs) are different again from those of either centrally planned or developed capitalist economies. The practical problems are enormous. Many LDCs have an acute shortage of trained staff. Computing systems are often impractical given the lack of finance, qualified staff and sometimes even a reliable power supply. There is often a need to direct attention to such special fields as farm accounting, bank accounting and industrial development accounting. The various elements of the economic system – enterprises, public administration and macro-economic planning – must be coordinated if an LDC is to follow a successful programme of economic development, and such cooperation implies reliable accounting information on a standardized basis. Unfortunately most of these countries rely on accounting methods which have evolved in a quite different economic environment. There is an urgent need for accountants to meet the challenge of measuring economic performance in LDCs.

We have already hinted at our final point of comparison between accounting as the language of economic activity and a living language such as English. Archaic words fall into disuse and are found only in the larger editions of the Oxford English Dictionary; others change their meaning or gain new meanings as a consequence of economic, technological and social change. Accounting practices and techniques are not static. As an accounting student I spent some time and effort learning the accounting entries for dealing with the forfeiture of shares in a limited company. In fact this procedure had already fallen into disuse in company practice and is now completely obsolete. On the other hand, there have been many important developments in accounting techniques over the past twenty years. For instance, advances in computer technology have revolutionized the task of processing and analysing data and have led to the development of new financial modelling techniques for evaluating the consequences of alternative courses of action.

The development of accounting

This view of accounting as a dynamic subject does not conflict with the observation that many present-day accounting practices can be traced back in history and often have their origins in quite different social and economic contexts. Here again, the analogy with language is obvious. It is impossible to describe what accounting is and (possibly more important) what it is in the process of becoming, without tracing the main developments in accounting practice over the centuries. This will be our task for the remainder of this chapter. The constant theme will be the close relationship between changes in accounting practice and changes in economic organization, technology and the requirements of users of accounting information.

Rudimentary forms of accounting can be traced back to the early civilizations of the Near East. As the inscriptions on Assyrian friezes and Egyptian pyramids witness, the rulers of these powerful states were obsessed with keeping lists which recorded their power and wealth – lists of soldiers, captives, cattle, and so on. The next step would be to record total expenditure on a particular project or the taxation levied by a ruler. These 'accounts' would still be in the form of simple lists, but would show values rather than a physical count. The practice of keeping such financial records became widespread in Greek and Roman times and with it the basic idea of 'keeping an account'.

In AD 73, Cicero delivered a speech against a governor of Sicily who was accused of misappropriation. 'We hear that some men never keep accounts', he said, but added 'There may be people who behave like this but it is not at all proper'.

Apart from listing receipts and payments, the idea of keeping an account also implies recording indebtedness. In medieval England, because parchment was expensive and many traders were unable to read, the practice developed of recording transactions on notched sticks or tallies. The size of the notches represented different values. As a writer in 1176 explained: '. . .the cut for £1 is the thickness of a grain of barley – a penny is marked by a single cut, nothing being removed.' After inscription, the tally was split down most of its length and each party took a section as a record of the transaction.

When the two sections were rejoined they would match exactly and so constitute proof of the debt. The same matching concept is used today when I key in my personal identification number at a bank cash dispenser. The computer will only allow me to draw cash if this number tallies with the information contained on my cash card and on the bank's computer file. Although tallies were used in private transactions, their main use was to record the public debts of the Exchequer. They continued in use into the eighteenth century, by which time they had become an anachronism. Tally sticks went out in a blaze of glory – literally. In 1834 it was decided to destroy the tallies kept in the basements at Westminster Hall. Once started, the fire got out of control and the whole of the old Parliament buildings were burned to the ground.

Another fundamental concept in accounting is that of having to 'account for' your activities. This notion of stewardship was evident in biblical times, as we may see from the parable of the talents. A servant or steward entrusted with his master's property or money would have to render periodic accounts of how it was used and what balances were still held. Although this idea is of ancient origin, the practice of stewardship accounting was developed most fully on the great monastic estates in the Middle Ages – probably the most efficient form of economic organization of the time. Religious orders could not, of course, 'own' property. Every member of the order would be required to account to his superior and, as members of the clergy had an effective monopoly of learning and literacy, it is natural that these accounts should be well kept in written form.

We have to look to Renaissance Italy to find the origins of modern business accounting methods. Trading is the most basic form of business activity and Italian cities such as Genoa, Florence and Venice were centres of expanding trade from around the twelfth century. Merchants bought and sold goods, often shipped from the East, and needed to keep accounts of each separate voyage in a systematic manner. This was particularly so with the advent of partnerships and joint ventures. Full records of the interests of the different parties to a venture would need to be kept and a method of calculating and apportioning profits which would be acceptable to all parties was required. Increasing use of credit, and the conduct of trade through agents, made it essential that accountability between debtors and creditors was reliable.

Double-entry book-keeping began to emerge in the fourteenth century as the answer to some of these accounting problems. The period of account would relate to the venture rather than to a regular time interval, such as one year. The accounts were closed off at the end of the venture to show how profitable it had been. This practice was well established when, in 1494, Luca Pacioli, a Franciscan friar, teacher and scholar, published a comprehensive treatise on mathematics which included a section dealing with methods of keeping accounts, setting out in a logical manner for the first time the system which was becoming accepted practice in Italy.

Although Pacioli's main interest in book-keeping was as an academic mathematician, his book was instrumental in spreading the 'Italian method' to other parts of Europe during the next two hundred years or so – a period when the centre of commercial influence was also moving westwards and northwards from Italy to Holland and England. The practice of setting up in business to undertake specific ventures gradually diminished and, with business units having a greater continuity in prospect, the trend towards periodic profit calculations developed. It is a tribute to the Italians' ingenuity that, despite many refinements, it is basically their system which has continued to the present day to provide the means for recording transactions, though the context and nature of the entries have changed to a degree that the Italians could not possibly have imagined.

Like many important ideas, the principle behind double-entry accounting is very simple. Every economic transaction can be expressed as an exchange and every exchange can be described in terms of a value given for a value received. The accounting records of an economic transaction should reflect this duality.

Suppose I buy a car for £3,000, paying by cheque. From my point of view this transaction has two counterbalancing elements: the receipt of a car worth £3,000 (to me) and the reduction of my bank balance by £3,000. I must record these two sides of the transaction in two separate accounts in my books. Bank (an asset account) should be reduced by £3,000 and motor vehicles (another asset account) increased by £3,000. If I sell merchandise on credit to Leonardo for £500, sales (an income account) has been increased and an asset account (Leonardo's debt to me) has also been increased by £500 to reflect the fact that he is now my debtor for this amount. Every conceivable economic transáction can also be analysed into two constituent elements. In every case an increase or decrease in one asset, liability, expense or income account will be exactly offset by a compensating entry in another account.

The adoption of the double-entry method of recording transactions has important practical benefits for a business. No matter how many transactions take place in an accounting period, it is possible to make a provisional check on the accuracy of the records. If there are two counterbalancing entries for each separate transaction, the sums of the entries for a set of transactions must also counterbalance. This simple arithmetical check is known as taking a trial balance. Apart from checking the consistency of the system, it is also possible to present the interrelated accounts of assets, liabilities, expenses and income in a way that will give valuable information about the state of the business. The method allows the bookkeeper to extract a profit and loss account and a balance sheet from the records kept within the accounting system.

Other important developments in accounting practice followed in the wake of industrialization. In England by the end of the eighteenth century, the domestic system of manufacture by outworkers was gradually being superseded by factory production. Equipping and manning these factories, extracting raw materials and transporting both materials and goods all required a larger scale of operations and, consequently, more investment. Capital beyond the resources of the entrepreneurs was required but others could not be expected to subscribe to such enterprises unless they knew that their liability was limited to the extent of their investment. Prospective investors in a company would also need to be assured that the prospectus inviting them to apply for shares was not grossly misleading and that when the company was formed its affairs would be subject to a reasonable degree of legal control. Such protection began to be provided from the middle of the nineteenth century by legislation which created limited liability status for subscribers to registered companies (1855) and then, by a series of consolidating Acts from 1862, extended the regulation of company affairs – a process which has continued ever since.

The emergence of accountancy as a separate profession was the necessary first step towards the formulation of acceptable codes of accounting practice. By the beginning of the nineteenth century, it was common practice for lawyers to employ specialists in the preparation of financial statements for bankrupt estates. A series of Bankruptcy Acts from 1825, together with the ever-growing financial tasks associated with companies and other statutory undertakings, rapidly increased the demand for such professional accounting services. By the second half of the nineteenth century there were enough accountants for them to form societies in some regions and, through a process of successive amalgamations, the professional bodies as we know them today came into existence. The Institute of Chartered Accountants in England and Wales, for instance, was incorporated in 1880. As the number and scale of business undertakings continued to grow, so did the number of professionally qualified accountants. The introduction of compulsory audit and the increasing scope of taxation were further reasons for the rapid growth of the profession. Originally auditors were a group of shareholders chosen from their own number at the Annual General Meeting. It soon became apparent that the employment of professional accountants as independent specialist auditors was a more efficient method of doing the job.

Financial accounting systems are mainly directed towards the control of resources and reporting of results, particularly with the interests of the owners in mind. Procedures for collecting and reporting costs of production have developed alongside financial accounting systems. Historically, such cost accounting systems grew out of the desire of manufacturers to find out the true cost of their products and to check that selling prices covered expenses and provided an adequate profit. During the eighteenth century, manufacturing in factories emerged as a more efficient method of organization than the traditional domestic system of putting out work to be done in the workers' own homes. These factories were not large by modern standards but raised entirely fresh problems of management to the new breed of entrepreneurs that brought them into being. These early factory owners appreciated the need to analyse costs. For instance Josiah Wedgwood, the great innovator in the pottery industry, admitted in 1776 that he had been '. . .puzzling my brain all the last week to find out proper data and methods of calculating the expenses of manufacture, sales and loss, etc., to be laid upon each article of manufacture, but without success'.

However, this failure to evolve adequate costing techniques in the early Industrial Revolution was not, by itself, critical to business success or failure. At that time the selling prices of the leading manufacturers tended to be so far above total costs, no matter how calculated, that almost any pricing policy was bound to earn a surplus. By the last quarter of the nineteenth century, however, international competition was more intense and managers were forced to look closely at costs of production to ensure that an adequate profit was being earned. At the same time, industrial organization was becoming more complex and manufacturers often produced a wider range of goods than the entrepreneurs of the early Industrial Revolution, such as Arkwright, Wedgwood and Watt. Costing systems were installed to analyse the material, labour and overhead costs associated with these complex activities in some detail. The apportionment of overheads to products was a particularly difficult problem and the total product costs which were reported by these systems were bound to be somewhat arbitrary. The 1914–18 war gave a further impetus to the development of cost accounting techniques. The government needed to control the cost of armaments and war supplies, particularly when these were supplied by contractors on a 'cost plus' basis, and so it required all contractors to keep proper records of their costs.

The period since the 1939–45 war has seen the most far-reaching changes in accounting methods and practice. There has been growing recognition of ways in which accounting could contribute to management decision-making: as accountants in industry and commerce became more closely involved as members of management teams, cost accounting evolved into management accounting. The post-war period has also seen the decline of such traditional industries as textiles, ship-building or coal mining and the growth of science-based industries and various service industries. The basic ideas of cost and management accounting have been applied in many new situations and practice has had to adapt to these changes in economic organization.

This rapid survey of accounting history from the earliest times to the present day has tried to emphasize the relationship between accounting practice and its economic, social and technological environment. As it is a commonplace to suggest that we are now living in a time of great change, it is hardly surprising that accounting practice is also evolving to keep pace with these changes.

The remaining chapters of this short book attempt to give an indication of how the subject of accounting is developing and how accountants are responding to the challenge of change in the modern world.

2

Business Accounting: a case study

In the previous chapter we introduced some of the problems of accounting practice by looking at a hypothetical set of personal accounts. Of course, few of us would wish to go into such detail in managing our financial affairs; the main reason for this survey was to establish some general principles which could then be applied to accounting for such complex organizations as a modern business corporation.

In this chapter we shall try to develop this parallel between personal and business accounting by looking at extracts from the annual published accounts of a well-known public limited company – the Burton Group plc. Although these extracts contain a number of technical accounting terms which cannot be explained in detail in this brief survey, the general principles should be clear enough. At least the study of an actual set of accounts rather than a textbook example emphasizes the point that accounting is a practical activity concerned with decisions in the real world. Obviously the actual published accounts contain a great deal more detail, partly to meet legal and other requirements but also to present additional information which the directors think will be of interest to the shareholders.

The Burton Group are clothing retailers selling in both the menswear and womenswear markets. They also have small manufacturing, distribution and credit card divisions which serve the main retailing divisions, which include such well-known High Street stores as Burton, Top Shop, Dorothy Perkins, Peter Robinson and Evans. The extracts are taken from the 1983 consolidated accounts which bring together the separate accounts of all these subsidiaries to give an overview of the Group's activities.

This survey of aspects of business accounting is divided into six sections, each of which is related to the earlier discussions of reasons for keeping personal accounts.

Profit and loss account

The business equivalent to my personal income and expenditure account is the profit and loss account. Table 1 shows how the Burton Group profit for the year is calculated and what the Board is recommending to do with it.

Table 1: Consolidated profit and loss account for the 52 weeks ended 27 August 1983 for the Burton Group plc and subsidiaries

	1983 £000
Turnover	299,174
Cost of sales	(238,918)
Gross profit	60,256
Distribution costs	(6,892)
Administrative expenses	(15,624)
Trading profit	37,740
Interest and similar income	1,168
Other income	215
Profit before taxation	39,123
Taxation	(11,000)
Dividends	(8,628)
Retained earnings	19,495

The Burton Group is essentially a trading organization purchasing menswear and womenswear from manufacturers for resale to the public. The difference between the Group's turnover (mainly sales of merchandise) and the cost of merchandise sold is the gross profit generated by these trading activities – £60.3m during the financial year. Distribution and administrative costs must be deducted from this figure and non-trading income added to it to arrive at a net figure or profit before taxation of £39.1m. This is the equivalent of the surplus which an individual or a club would hope to generate from their current activities and which they would record in an income and expenditure account.

The rest of the account shows what happens to this profit. £11m goes to the Inland Revenue, mainly in the form of corporation tax, £8.6m is distributed to shareholders as dividends and the remainder (£19.4m) is in effect corporate saving. These retained earnings will be ploughed back to generate profit in future years.

How are we to assess the Group's success? A profit of £39.1m before taxation sounds a large amount but needs to be related to other information before we can pass a judgement. Table 2 shows that profits have increased over the last three years, well in excess of the rate of inflation. Table 2 also shows two sets of ratios, one relating profit to turnover and the other to capital employed by the business. The return on capital employed is particularly significant. Each shareholder has made an investment in the company and this ratio tells him whether the rate of return on his investment is satisfactory. If the rate of return is too low he would have done better to have put his money in a relatively risk-free form of saving, such as a building society deposit account. In fact, these two measures clearly indicate a strong upward trend in profitability. In his statement which accompanies the accounts, the Chairman is clearly right to claim that 1982–3 was another successful year for the Burton Group.

Table 2: Profit trends over three years for the Burton Group plc and subsidiaries

	1981	1982	1983
Profit before taxation	£16.4m	£24.3m	£39.1m
Trading profit as a percentage of turnover	8.7	10.5	12.6
Percentage return on capital employed	11.8	11.2	16.4

Balance sheet

Our earlier discussion showed how I might draw up my personal balance sheet by listing and valuing my assets and liabilities to show my net financial position at a particular date. Similar principles of balance sheet construction apply to a large business enterprise, even though the sums involved are

much larger and the practical accounting problems more difficult. Table 3 sets out the Balance Sheet of the Burton Group to
show the net assets or capital employed by the business at 27
August 1983. As in the case of my personal balance sheet the
assets are grouped into fixed and current assets. A distinction
is also drawn between liabilities due within a year (current
liabilities) and long term liabilities.

**Table 3: Consolidated Balance Sheet at 27 August 1983 for the Burton
Group plc and subsidiaries**

	£'000	£'000
Fixed assets		
Freehold property	92,196	
Leasehold property	101,790	
Branch assets	41,635	
Investments	11,780	
		247,401
Current assets		
Stocks	38,373	
Debtors	12,350	
Investments	2,064	
Bank balances and cash	18,933	
	71,720	
Less current liabilities		
(creditors due within one year)	66,479	
		5,241
Net current assets		252,642
Long term liabilities		
Debenture loans	4,736	
Taxation	2,997	
Provision for liabilities		
and charges	5,853	
		13,586
Capital employed (net assets)		239,056
Represented by		
Called up share capital		43,079
Reserves		195,977
		239,056

The most important fixed assets of the Burton Group are its freehold and leasehold properties: mainly retail stores located in valuable High Street sites. A valuation based on the original cost of these properties would be meaningless and so the balance sheet figure for freehold and long leasehold properties is based on a full revaluation made at the beginning of the current accounting period. Branch assets include such items as fixtures and fittings, office equipment and motor vehicles. These are all depreciating assets which will be valued in the balance sheet at less than their original cost. The figure of £41.6m shown in the balance sheet is therefore the net book value after providing for depreciation.

In contrast with the group's fixed assets, current assets (cash, debtors, stock) and current liabilities (creditors) are constantly changing. Most of these movements are directly related to the day to day trading activities of the business. Goods are bought on credit from suppliers (creditors) and then sold to customers, either for cash or on credit (debtors). The cash generated by these activities is used to pay wages and other expenses and settle accounts with creditors. Other payments and receipts not associated with the trading cycle, such as dividend and tax payments, will also have to be met. Figure 1 opposite shows how the net current assets of the business (£5.2m) are used to generate profits.

In Chapter 1 we used a number of analogies to explain the nature of accounting practice. The operations of the trading cycle and its effect on the accounts listed in the balance sheet can also be represented as a simple analogy. In a plumbing system, various tanks and cisterns designed to contain water are connected together by pipes through which water flows. The level of water in any given tank is determined by the net effect of the flows into and out of the tank. It follows that the total volume of the water in all the tanks of the system will be determined by the rates of flow in and out of the system. In the same way there is a logical relationship between income and expenditure (flow) accounts and asset and liability (level) accounts. The closing balances of asset accounts are equivalent to the recorded levels of the tanks and cisterns in a plumbing system. Of course, the analogy breaks down when we consider liability accounts such as trade creditors, unless we can imagine a group of negative tanks where outflows

The Burton Group

Trading cycle

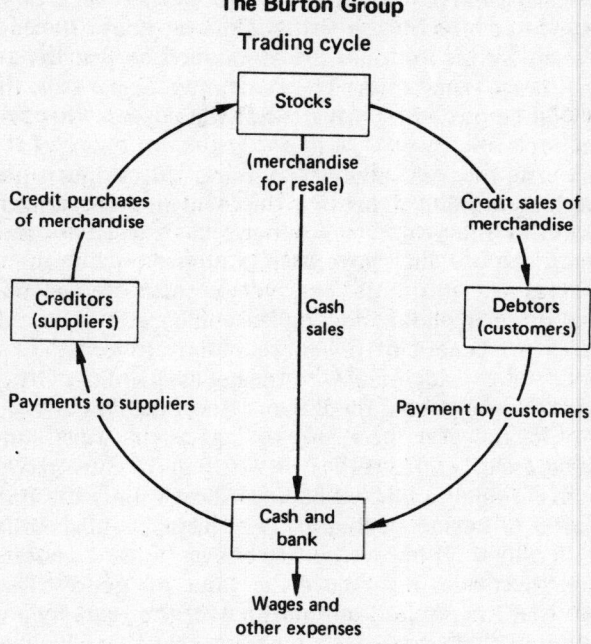

Figure 1

exceed inflows! So far as the system as a whole is concerned, the principle is clear. Provided that we ignore taxation and dividend payments, an increase in profit during the year would be reflected by an identical increase in the company's net assets.

The Burton Group Balance Sheet (Table 3) reports a figure of £239m as the capital employed by the business by offsetting current and long term liabilities against fixed and current assets. If for a moment we accept that this figure represents a view of the company's worth, who actually 'owns' these net assets? The Burton Group as a public limited company is a separate legal entity owned by its shareholders. The company has a called up share capital of £43,079,537 which is made up of 86,159,074 shares of 50p each nominal value. Who are these shareholders? Information provided in the accounts shows that directors and their families own about eight per cent of the shares. Most of the Burton Group's shares (about 70 per cent) are owned by institutional investors such as pension funds and insurance companies. The remaining 22 per cent of the shares will be owned by private individuals and other limited companies.

Of course, the true value of the shareholders' investment in the company is much higher than the £43m nominal value of the shares. Over the years the company has earned substantial profits, much of which have been ploughed back in the form of reserves. A substantial reserve was also created on the revaluation of freehold and long leaseholds. All these reserves accrue to the benefit of the shareholders. Indeed the shareholders' 'stake' is identical with the net assets of the Group as shown in the top part of the Balance Sheet (£239m).

It would, however, be wrong to suggest that this figure of £239m necessarily reflects the true worth of the Burton Group. The conventional published balance sheet is only the start of the subject of business valuation. For instance, in accordance with generally accepted accounting conventions, the published Balance Sheet does not record the value of 'goodwill'. It is obvious that the reputation built up over the years by a well-known retail chain store has a high market value which could be realized, if necessary, if the group decided to sell off one or more of its divisions. Customer goodwill, staff skills and good industrial relations are not easy to value in hard cash terms, even though they are essential for success in business.

What is the company really worth? One answer might be to look at the stock market valuation of the shares. On 1 September 1983 the ordinary shares of the Burton Group were quoted at 322p per share. At that date, therefore, the total market capitalization of the shares was:

$$86m \times 322p = £277m$$

Whether this market capitalization represents the true worth of the company is, of course, a matter of opinion. By 13 June 1984 the market price of the shares had fallen to 270p per share to give a total market capitalization of £233m. Much of this fall in value could be attributed to uncertainty caused by high interest rates in the USA and worries about a long miners' strike in the United Kingdom. These factors weakened general business confidence which in turn affected the market's view of the Burton Group's future earning potential.

Short term financial management

The company should have no problems in meeting its commitments. The company is generating substantial regular cash receipts from its profitable trading activities and so should be able to plan cash payments, even when these include large seasonal items such as dividend and corporation tax payments. Published company accounts must include a 'Source and Application of Funds' statement which, as the name implies, describes where cash has come from and what use has been made of it over the year.

During 1983 the principal changes in the Burton Group's funds were as follows:

	£m
Opening cash balances	11
Generated from operations	48
Capital expenditure	(29)
Tax and dividends	(10)
Working capital and other items	(2)
Closing cash balances	18

Over the year the level of cash balances had increased from £11m to £18m. The cash generated from current operations was applied to pay tax and dividends, build up stocks and build up cash balances. The largest part, however, was ploughed back into capital investment to secure future growth for the business. When introducing short term financial planning at the personal level we noted the need to avoid large idle cash balances. Because the Burton Group has experienced such a large increase in its 'liquid' resources, it has decided to invest £2m of these funds during 1983 in shares and other securities. Unfortunately, conditions on the stock market were not buoyant and at the balance sheet date the market value of these investments had fallen to £1.6m.

Long term financial planning

The Source and Application of Funds statement summarized above shows clearly that the Group is taking advantage of the funds generated from current operations to increase substantially the level of investment in fixed assets. This capital expenditure of £29.3m represents a 74 per cent increase on the previous year. The trading space of the Group has been increased by over 130,000 square feet. A total of 55 new sites were opened during the year whilst 19 shops were re-sited and seven extended.

The Burton Group is in the fortunate position of being able to finance its current long term plans by ploughing back current profits. In other circumstances the company might have to raise long term finance either by increasing its debenture loans or by floating a new issue of shares to the public. An examination of the long term liabilities section of the Balance Sheet (Table 3) shows that, in the past, the Group has raised finance through debenture loans (£4.7m outstanding in 1983). These debentures are fixed interest loans, redeemable at various dates between 1986 and 2003. Another possible method of raising finance is by floating a new issue of shares on the stock market. There is an important difference between shares and debentures. Ordinary shareholders do not receive a fixed rate of interest but, as members of the company, they are entitled to participate in its profits if any are made. For 1983, for instance, the directors are recommending the payment of a total dividend of 10p per 50p share, which compares with 7.75p per share in 1982.

A company wishing to raise additional finance from the market has to give very careful consideration to the options open to it. For instance, a new debenture loan will commit the company to annual fixed interest payments, regardless of the profit position. On the other hand, a new issue of ordinary shares will dilute the ownership of the company with the risk that control might pass into other hands. Here again we can echo the comments made when introducing personal financial planning. Companies, as well as individuals, need to seek out the most attractive sources of finance, minimize the cost of that finance and secure the best tax advantage.

Management accounts

The annual report and accounts of a public limited company are intended to be read by shareholders. The management accounts which are produced within the organization are not publicly available; they are intended to help the managers improve the efficiency of current operations and plan for the future. The published profit and loss account reports the overall results of the year's activities. In the management accounts a detailed breakdown of costs and profits is needed to show how the various activities contribute to the total profit of the group.

Table 4: Turnover and profit by activity for the Burton Group plc and subsidiaries

	Turnover		Profit	
	1983 £'000	increase on 1982	1983 £'000	increase on 1982
Retailing		%		%
Menswear	155,202	+28	23,272	+49
Womenswear	139,198	+31	14,166	+64
Total retailing	294,400	+29	37,438	+54
Manufacturing	591		91	
Other activities	4,183		211	
Turnover and trading profit	299,174	+29	37,740	+55
Interest			1,168	
Other income			215	
	1983 £'000	increase on 1982	1983 £'000	increase on 1982
Profit before taxation			39,123	+61

Note: Divisions are charged with their share of the costs of running the Group and are credited with their share of income from the Group's property and credit operations.

In fact, the published accounts do provide us with a broad analysis of sales and profitability between the Group's principal activities (see Table 4). The menswear divisions, Burton and Top Man, together increased profits by 49 per cent. The womenswear divisions, Top Shop, Dorothy Perkins, Evans and Peter Robinson, achieved a total increase of 64 per cent. These increases in profits were significantly higher than increases in turnover during the same period. The improvement in profitability of the womenswear divisions was particularly strong.

The internal management accounts will, of course, analyse results in much greater detail. The intention would be to allocate and apportion all the costs incurred by the business to the various activities in whatever detail is necessary, for example to branches or to lines of merchandise. A fashion business must introduce new ranges and develop existing ranges if it is to survive and expand. All lines of merchandise will be costed and their profitability assessed. One particular difficulty faced by cost accountants is the apportionment of common costs incurred by the business as a whole to separate activites. If, for instance, the management of British Leyland wish to know the cost of a Maestro, they must include not only the obvious costs of raw materials, component parts and the wages of production workers, but also a proportion of those indirect costs which may seem rather remote from the business of actually making the car. Take, for instance, the wages of the commissionaire at the factory gate. This is an example of a common cost incurred for the benefit of the company as a whole rather than for one particular model of car. A true cost of the Maestro must, however, include a proportion of his wages. The note below the Burton Group plc analysis of turnover and profits is another example of the apportionment of common costs. In this case, however, both costs and income relating to the Group as a whole are shared between the various divisions. Such apportionments of common costs can be somewhat arbitrary and although useful for some purposes the results may be positively misleading if used to guide some management decisions. In the discussion of car expenses in Chapter 1 a distinction was made between fixed and variable costs. This distinction is of crucial importance in management accounting. Expenses such as rates will be fixed no matter what level of sales are achieved by the business. If sales are low, the dead weight of these fixed costs will probably mean that the business is unable to break even.

Decision accounting

A business decision is a unique event, whether it is a decision to open a new branch, lease or buy a computer, fix the selling price of a garment or drop an existing line from the range. When making a decision, managers will need to select from the mass of available data whatever information is appropriate for the decision. All the relevant costs and benefits for a complete evaluation of the proposal must be estimated and this information will be produced specially for use in making that particular decision. Routine accounting reports will be of limited value for this purpose because these usually record past costs and benefits, whereas a decision relates to future events: for example, what will be the effect on profits over the next few years of a decision to introduce a new range of menswear?

Let us take a relatively simple business decision which in some respects is parallel to the choice of method of travelling to work discussed in Chapter 1. A production manager in the manufacturing division has to decide whether or not to scrap an existing machine and replace it with a new one costing £25,000. The old machine cost £12,000 five years ago and, as it is being depreciated at £1,000 per annum, its 'written down' value is now £7,000. The production manager must decide whether the estimated future benefits from installing the new machine will justify the outlay of £25,000. In reaching his decision, he should not be influenced by the original cost of the old machine (£12,000). This is a committed or 'sunk' cost and nothing to be decided now will alter that fact. The annual depreciation charge should also be ignored because depreciation is essentially an accounting device to apportion the original cost of the machine over its estimated life. On the other hand, the estimated future running costs of the old machine will need to be included in the comparison. There is no commitment to these future running costs; they may be avoided if the old machine is scrapped and the new machine installed. Any scrap value of the old machine would have to be included. The golden rule is to make sure that only relevant costs and benefits are included in the appraisal; future costs are relevant but sunk costs must be ignored.

Of course, many business decisions are more complex than this simple machine replacement problem. For instance, in 1983 Burtons introduced the new Top Girl range aimed at 'fashionable 9 to 14-year-olds' into the Top Shop division. Before the managers decided to launch the range they would need to conduct extensive market research as well as consider the financial implications of this new venture. The business is a total system and finance cannot be separated from technical, marketing and personnel aspects.

Let us look at some of the major long term decisions which have been taken by our case study company. In the past, Burtons had substantial manufacturing interests but, some years ago, a decision was taken to concentrate on retailing and to diversify into womenswear from its traditional base in menswear. An earlier decision to set up a French subsidiary was not successful and in 1980 the Group sold this interest. At the present time the Board is looking forward to a major expansion in the Group's activities. The total value of the clothing market in the United Kingdom in 1983 was £8.5 billion, an increase of eight per cent over the previous year. The Burton Group has only four per cent of this market; three per cent of womenswear and five per cent of menswear. The Board sees considerable growth potential in both these markets and is backing its judgement with a substantial capital investment programme. Business accountants have a crucial role to play when strategic decisions are being made by the board of a company. They are in the best position to estimate the costs of the various courses of action under consideration and to advise on alternative methods of financing.

In the next chapter we shall examine more closely the duties undertaken by accountants and the skills and qualities they need to carry out their responsibilities. We shall, of course, need to look at professional accounting practice and public service accounting as well as the tasks of business accounting that we have met in the case study of the Burton Group.

3

The compleat accountant

Mr Smeeth had sufficient routine work to carry him through the morning, but he felt queerly insecure, not at all happy with his books, his neat little figures, his pencil, rubber, blue ink and red ink, now that he no longer knew what was happening to the firm. It was like trying to post a ledger swinging above a dark gulf.

J.B. Priestley: *Angel Pavement*

The accounting profession

The ways of becoming a professional accountant in the United Kingdom are many and various and it is not this book's intention to enter into detail about routes towards professional qualification, although a brief summary is included as Appendix C. Our aim is rather to examine the qualities required by a successful accountant, look at the work undertaken by accountants and, in passing, see how the profession is organized in the United Kingdom.

Accountants have never had a particularly favourable image with the public at large; accounting is not the most glamorous of occupations. The stereotype of an accountant is a 'John Cleese' figure – bureaucratic, boring and blinkered. No doubt such accountants do exist but then there are probably some boring airline pilots! It should be apparent from our discussion of accounting in the previous chapters that at least the work itself should not be boring. Admittedly, the trainee accountant must expect to undertake some fairly tedious work: checking invoices as part of an audit routine for example. At the same time computers have taken much of the drudgery out of the processing and analysis of accounting information undertaken by accounts clerks and accounting 'technicians'. So far as the professional accountant is concerned, I have tried to emphasize the creative aspects of the work. Whether accountants work in industry, commerce, public authority or in public practice, they need flair and imagination as well as the more obvious qualities of reliability and integrity.

Students leaving school and considering accounting as a career will need some determination to study accounting in depth on a relevant degree course, then complete a period of training lasting three years whilst studying for the professional examinations. But what are the special skills and aptitudes which are necessary if our aspirants are ever to become effective members of the profession?

It is self-evident that accountants must be numerate. This does not mean that prospective accountants need necessarily be mathematical prodigies. It is perhaps unfortunate that careers teachers in schools often assume that all students who have done well at mathematics, but who are not necessarily strong on the sciences or arts subjects, would, by a process of elimination, be suitable candidates for the accounting profession. There is more to being an accountant than the ability to understand calculus! Indeed, it is worth examining rather more closely what we mean by numeracy in this context. The ability to add up columns of figures accurately is valuable but of marginal relevance in the age of cheap calculators. Although the ability to understand mathematical reasoning is, as we have seen, an important aspect of higher education courses in accounting, an engineer or a scientist needs to study advanced mathematics in greater depth. In terms of the day to day work of a practising accountant, the ability to understand quickly the significance of a mass of information presented in quantitative form is of crucial significance. This is a distinctive numeracy skill, separate from the skills of computation and mathematical reasoning. Readers may wish to test their own financial comprehension skills by looking at Table 5 on page 39 from the Burton Group's published accounts. What major trends may be discerned over this five year period? Which are the key figures and which figures can be glossed over on a quick reading in order to obtain an overall picture? What is the significance of the ratios? Are there any other important interrelationships?

In addition to producing information, the accountant must

be an effective communicator of that information. The accountant who churns out, or allows the computer to churn out, voluminous reports which are read by few and understood by none is hardly an effective communicator. Intended meanings can become distorted in the communication process. 'Send reinforcements, I'm going to advance' becomes 'Send three and fourpence, I'm going to a dance'. The reported unit cost of widgets during January is based on a number of

Table 5: Five year review of the Burton Group plc and subsidiaries

	1979 £'000	1980 £'000	1981 £'000	1982 £'000	1983 £'000
Group turnover	163,830	213,110	213,718	231,944	299,174
Trading profit	17,470	14,729	18,656	24,271	37,740
Interest	(2,335)	(5,224)	(4,128)	(128)	1,168
Other income	1,823	3,125	1,846	164	215
Profit before taxation	16,958	12,630	16,374	24,307	39,123
Taxation	(1,618)	(1,949)	(2,336)	(4,900)	(11,100)
Profit after taxation	15,340	10,681	14,038	19,407	28,023
Extraordinary items	3,424	(10,328)	2,027	—	—
Profit for the financial year	18,764	353	16,065	19,407	28,023
Dividends	(3,743)	(4,262)	(5,193)	(6,460)	(8,628)
Retained earnings	15,021	(3,909)	10,872	12,947	19,395
Tangible assets and investments	158,895	172,087	161,682	226,188	247,401
Current assets less liabilities and provisions	(17,059)	(46,395)	(22,645)	(9,996)	(8,345)
Total assets employed	141,836	125,692	139,037	216,192	239,056
Share capital	18,601	38,742	39,933	41,544	43,079
Reserves	123,235	86,950	99,104	174,648	195,977
Capital employed	141,836	125,692	139,037	216,192	239,056

arbitrary assessments about stock valuation and the apportionment of fixed overheads to products. The accountant knows this but is the marketing manager, who may wish to use the figures as a basis for fixing the price of widgets, aware of the ambiguities contained in this reported cost information? Managers must be able to understand the meaning of various reports which they receive and have confidence in their value as a basis for action. The accountant must be able to prepare lucid reports. Reports on the performance of candidates in professional academic examinations frequently comment adversely on the ability of candidates to express themselves clearly in English. The ability to summarize a complex argument, present the main alternatives and submit a clear recommendation on the proverbial 'two sides of A4' is an invaluable skill.

A popular fallacy about accountants is that they are introverts who are happiest working alone in their offices, surrounded by reams of paper covered in weird hieroglyphics. Without arguing that accountants should be extroverts, it is important that they possess certain basic social skills. Accountants need to be sensitive to the needs of the organizations which they serve. Auditors investigating the systems of client companies need to muster all the skills of tact and diplomacy at their command and yet be firm in following through a line of enquiry. A budget accountant has to co-ordinate all the information coming from the production, marketing and other departments into a coherent financial plan. Genuine cooperation with the managers in setting their targets is essential if budgets are to be an effective management control.

We have already noted the existence of different specialisms in accounting work. There is first of all the broad classification between accountants in professional practice and those employed in industry, commerce and the public service. There is also a fair degree of specialization within these groups. For instance, although some small chartered accountant and certified accountant practices operate as 'general practitioners', most accountants in professional practice tend to concentrate on either auditing or taxation work. Indeed some accountants operate in very specialized areas: liquidation, bankruptcy and receivership, for example. Most accountants working in industry will also specialize in either financial accounting, financial management or management accounting.

On first sight it would appear that the accounting profession in the United Kingdom is organized on the basis of specialisms, some bodies catering for professional accountants in practice, with specialist groups of management accountants and public service accountants. In practice, however, there is considerable overlap, not to say confusion. Before we look more closely at the work done by these three main groups of accountants, let us take a brief look at the formal structure of the profession. The six recognized accountancy bodies are:–

The Institute of Chartered Accountants in England and Wales (ICAEW)
The Chartered Association of Certified Accountants (ACA)
The Institute of Cost and Management Accountants (ICMA)
The Institute of Chartered Accountants of Scotland (ICAS)
The Chartered Institute of Public Finance and Accountancy (CIPFA)
The Institute of Chartered Accountants in Ireland (ICAI)

There was an abortive attempt to integrate these six bodies in the early 1970s. There have been no further attempts at full integration since then, although the six bodies cooperate through joint committees on such matters as setting accounting standards (SSAPs). We shall summarize the aims and objectives of each of these six bodies in turn.

There are three separate institutes of Chartered Accountants for England and Wales, Scotland and Ireland. In fact the Scottish institute is the oldest established body, as the predecessor societies in Edinburgh and Glasgow were formed and received their Royal Charters in the 1850s. The Institute of Chartered Accountants in England and Wales was formed in 1880 and is the largest of the six bodies: indeed, more than half of the total qualified accountants in the British Isles are ICAEW members. The Irish Institute is organized to cater for the needs of accountants in both the Republic of Ireland and Northern Ireland. All members of the three chartered institutes must undergo a period of training with an existing member in a practising office; consequently they carry out most of the 'professional' accounting work. Although most people think of chartered accountants as working in practising offices, the majority now work outside practice, carrying out a wide range of roles in industry, commerce, the public service and other types of organization.

Most members of the Chartered Association of Certified Accountants work in industry, public corporations or commerce. A small number who have trained in public practice and have obtained the necessary practising certificate are also engaged in practice. As the name implies, most members of the Institute of Cost and Management Accountants specialize in management accounting. The institute was founded in 1919 as the Institute of Cost and Works Accountants. The change in name shows how management accounting has developed in this century. Costing began as a technique in factory administration but the growth of service industries has led to the widespread use of management accounting methods in all types of organizations, public and private. The Chartered Institute of Public Finance and Accounting is a small group of accountants who work mainly in local government, but also in other public service authorities – water and health authorities, for example.

The status of a professionally qualified accountant is limited to full membership of one of these six recognized bodies. There is, however, a considerable body of work which does not necessarily call for full professional skills. Jobs as audit clerks and supervisors of sections of a cost department are two examples of work which might be undertaken by such accounting technicians. In the United Kingdom the main accounting bodies have sponsored a separate body called the Association of Accounting Technicians (AAT) to help meet the growing demand for education and training below the full professional level. The diploma and certificate courses organized under the aegis of the Business and Technician Education Council (BTEC) also help to meet this demand.

Although this discussion of the accounting profession has concentrated on the position in the British Isles, it would be wrong to forget the international dimension of accounting. Many chartered firms are part of international organizations with branches in the USA and many other parts of the world. Many accountants with British qualifications are to be found working overseas, partly as a consequence of the growth of multinational businesses, partly because of the wide spread of 'Anglo-Saxon' accounting practices in many parts of the world, but also because a British qualification is held in high esteem in both Western countries and the Third World. British membership of the EEC has also had an effect on accounting, particularly as a result of moves to harmonize company law and accounting. It is perhaps worth mentioning in passing that there is a strong demand for British accountants fluent in another major European language by both multinational business corporations and the large professional firms.

We shall now turn from the complexities of professional organizations to look at the actual jobs undertaken by accountants. We shall consider in turn the work of the practising accountant, the public service accountant and the accountant in business. Rather more time will be spent with business accounting, partly because most accountants work in industry or commerce but, more importantly, to emphasize the crucial link between accounting and management control.

Professional practice

An accountant in public practice will either work independently as a sole practitioner or as a partner in a practising firm; the professional bodies do not allow practices to be organized as limited liability companies. Some of the large firms of chartered accountants have many partners and several specialist departments covering different types of audit, taxation and management consultancy. For instance the Burton Group's accounts are audited by Price Waterhouse, one of the largest chartered firms with 70 partners (in 1982) and a total professional staff of 2,064.

Audit

By law, the accounts of a limited company must be audited by a properly qualified auditor who must be a member of one of four professional bodies recognized by the 1948 Companies Act to undertake this work (ICAEW, ICAS, ICAI, ACA) and who has been granted a practising certificate from the Department of Trade. From the legal point of view, auditors are appointed by the shareholders of the limited company and their fees have to be agreed at the Annual General Meeting. Accounts presented to the Annual General Meeting must include an auditor's report which gives an assurance to the shareholders that the various external requirements have been complied with, that proper books have been kept and that the accounts as a whole represent a true and fair view of the company's financial affairs. If the auditors feel unable to make a statement on these lines, they must 'qualify' the accounts. This only happens rarely and would usually be a matter for serious concern.

High audit standards are essential if the business community is to have confidence in the validity of published accounts. Before being able to certify the accounts the auditors must test the total system by following through sample transactions. In practice, most of the detailed routine checking is carried out by trainee accountants under the direction of qualified accountants following procedures laid down in an audit manual to ensure that the audit is conducted in a systematic manner. However, auditing is not merely a matter of detecting fraud and testing the security of an accounting system. Auditors are often in a position to give general advice about the organization of the client's business and it is not surprising that many of the larger firms of chartered accountants have their own management consultancy departments.

Taxation

Apart from being burdensome, British taxation is very complicated. The direct taxes levied on individuals include income tax, capital gains tax, capital transfer tax and investment income surcharge. Average citizens, whose main source of income is from employment, should be able to cope with their own tax assessments provided they make sure that they are claiming all the allowances to which they are entitled. Difficulties will arise with overseas earnings and income from self-employment, to give but two examples. In such cases the individual ought to consider taking professional advice from an accountant.

The tax rules affecting businesses can be very complicated and professional advice is usually necessary. Individuals in business on their own account or in partnership with others will pay income tax and other personal taxes on their profits or share of profits. The main tax levied on companies is corporation tax. For instance, almost all the £11.1m set aside in the Burton Group consolidated profit and loss account for taxation is in respect of anticipated corporation tax. It is clear that, with sums of this magnitude at stake, company accountants and their tax advisers must pay careful thought to tax planning.

A business pays tax on its profits, but the basis of tax assessment is not necessarily the net profit figure as calculated in the conventional profit and loss account. The Inland Revenue will not allow some expenses as a deduction for tax purposes – some business entertaining expenses, for example. In other cases there are rules governing the level of expenses which may be charged as is the case with depreciation allowances. For taxation purposes, assets are grouped into various categories such as plant and machinery and industrial buildings, and a standard rate of depreciation is fixed for each category of assets. As the rate of depreciation charged in the firm's books for its own purposes may well be different from the Inland Revenue's allowances, an adjustment to reported profits must be made when calculating the depreciation allowed for tax purposes.

The tax treatment of depreciation is a relatively simple matter. Many companies have to comply with rules of bewildering complexity about such matters as advance corporation tax, provision for carrying losses forward and income earned overseas. Company accountants and their professional tax advisers devote considerable time and ingenuity to making sure that the company's affairs are so arranged that the tax liability is minimized. Here is another area where the practising accountant must observe high standards of professional ethics. A line must be drawn between illegal tax evasion and legitimate tax avoidance.

Public service accounting

As we have implied elsewhere, central government accounting is something of an arcane mystery to all apart from those civil servants who practise it. The finances of central government are administered through a series of 'funds', the most important of which is the Consolidated Fund originally established by Pitt in 1787. Parliament authorizes appropriations from the Consolidated Fund to particular 'votes' or heads of account for a service. There are five separate votes for defence, for example. A senior civil servant acts as Accounting Officer for all the budget heads administered by a department and any unexpended balances must be passed back to the Consolidated Fund. Ultimately Parliament, through the Committee of Public Accounts, is responsible for the efficient working of this rather cumbersome system. More detailed day to day control is exercised by civil servants in the Treasury and the Comptroller and Auditor General must certify that the expenditure for each vote has been 'applied for the purposes authorized by Parliament'.

Local government in England and Wales is the responsibility of a large number of independent authorities, each providing a range of services within its area. County Councils, for instance, are responsible *inter alia* for education, social services, fire services, police and libraries. Apart from some trading income, they are financed partly by grants from central government and partly from rates levied on property in the area. Every year a County Council must prepare a budget which balances planned expenditure against revenue from all these sources. Once it is known how much must be raised from the ratepayers, the authority will fix a rate poundage, calculated by dividing the total budgeted rate revenue by the estimated rateable value of property in the area. Once fixed, the officers responsible for running a local government service will be expected to keep within it. It may be possible to reallocate sums between certain heads *within* a budget, but permission to exceed a total budget allocation normally requires special approval from the finance committee of the authority. Such a system is necessary if the authority is to avoid serious overspending. Local politicians do not wish to incur the displeasure of the electorate by increasing rates to cover past overspending. Local government accountants must monitor the spending of the service departments carefully to make sure that budgets are not exceeded without good cause. It is also necessary to make sure that all expenditure is *intra vires*, or within the powers, of the authority. In general, a local authority may only provide a particular type of service if it is empowered to do so by Act of Parliament. If the Councillors of Little Muddleton District Council decided to open a betting shop in their area, they would run the risk of having to meet the costs out of their own pocket. In the jargon of local government, they would be surcharged for the *ultra vires* expenditure.

It is difficult to evaluate the performance of public bodies by the usual commercial criteria of profitability. Public library services and police protection are not sold in the market and so it is not possible to calculate a return on capital employed, as was the case with the Burton Group plc. Public Service accountants have therefore devised various performance indicators, some of which indicate how efficiently the authority has been using its resources whilst others attempt to measure the quality or extent of the service provided. Some ratios can be interpreted in different ways. For instance, a fall in the pupil–teacher ratio in secondary schools from 16:1 to 15:1 may be seen as a worsening of teacher productivity or an improvement in the quality of education, depending on your point of view.

Management accounting

As we saw in Chapter 1, all activities, from my personal financial affairs to the management of the economy, need to be planned and controlled. The more complex the activity, the greater is the need for a carefully thought out plan. For instance, the modern automated methods of car production need years of planning by a variety of specialist 'technocrats'. Designers try to translate the public's requirements, as indicated by market research, into a production model. Prototypes are tested and, if satisfactory, production engineers design the special-purpose robots needed in modern computer-aided manufacturing systems. Materials requirements have to be planned in advance and, where possible, the purchasing department will enter into long term contracts with suppliers. Labour requirements will be shown in a manpower plan, which may indicate the need for recruitment and training, if shortages of particular skills are likely in the future. For instance, the Fiat Cassino plant near Naples only requires a workforce of 6,000 to produce 1,300 cars a day. Although some of these workers are unskilled or semi-skilled, an increasing proportion will need specialized skills; maintenance engineers, for example. Marketing has to be planned from the initial market research to advertising, selling and distributing the completed model. The accountant's contribution will be towards financial planning, financial control and assessing the profitability of the whole project.

As a first step in the planning process, long-range objectives must be set for the company. This process should raise fundamental questions about future development. What kind of business should the company be in? What share of the market is possible? What rates of profitability and growth should be achieved? How important are 'non-economic objectives' such as creating a favourable company image? The choice of objectives will be based on a close study of the present economic, social and political environment, and an assessment of future trends. For instance, as a result of such a survey, the management of a cigarette manufacturing company may conclude that the total market for cigarettes is stagnating. What is the company to do in order to meet its long term growth and profitability objectives? Should it adopt an aggressive marketing policy aimed at capturing a higher share of the cigarette market? Should it develop new products, such as cigars, which appear to be a faster-growing sector of the total tobacco market? Should it diversify into products such as potato crisps or soft drinks, which can be marketed through the same outlets as cigarettes? Should it move into something completely different, such as the leisure industry, if a higher rate of return on investment could be achieved by this strategy? In a rapidly changing world, companies must constantly ask themselves the basic question, 'What business are we in?'

After strategic planning for the company's long term future, the organization and information system must be planned to meet the changing administrative needs of this strategy. Finally, the day-to-day operations of the company need to be planned. Production, marketing, financing, manning, purchasing and all the other activites of the modern business, need to be co-ordinated into an operating plan. When expressed in financial terms, this operating plan becomes a budgetary control system.

Having set company objectives and prepared strategic, administrative and operating plans, management must make sure that the plans are either carried out, or altered in the light of changed circumstances. This is the function of control. However, it would be wrong to consider planning and control as separate activities; it is better to think of them as two aspects of a continuous management process.

It is perhaps easiest to see the principles at work in a simple mechanical control system. A room thermostat, for instance, keeps the air between two predetermined temperatures. A thermometer measures the temperature, and control is exercised by switching the current to the heater on or off, depending on which limit is reached.

However, management control differs in several respects from thermostatic control. In the first place an organization such as a business is a social system and human behaviour is not as easy to measure and control as the performance of a machine. An added complication is that a business is not a closed, static system like a thermostat, but an open system reacting to and dealing with its economic, social, legal and political environment. This environment is constantly changing, and the firm's plans must change with it.

What part do accountants play in the process of management control? In one sense they are concerned with the whole, because all plans have financial implications and nearly all the firm's activities will incur costs which must be accounted for. In practice their main concern will be with four aspects of the planning and control process:

1 the financial implications of *plans*;
2 the financial *measurement* of the firm's activities;
3 the *comparison* of actual costs and revenues with planned costs and revenues;
4 the *feedback* of information to management about significant deviations from plans, in financial terms.

Of course, the planning activities of the business are not simply accounting exercises. The formulation of the manpower plan, for instance, relies mainly on the application of specialized personnel management techniques. The accountant will need to be involved in any discussion of the financial implications of the plan, but many key concepts, such as the quality of labour skills and state of labour relations, cannot be expressed in financial terms. Performance is often measured in non-financial terms, for example by calculating rates of labour turnover and taking the 'stock' of various skills to see if they match planned requirements. Accounting information must be used in deciding whether the manpower plan has been achieved, but it is not the only source of control information. Similar observations could be made about research and development plans, marketing plans, strategic plans and administrative plans.

Another limitation of the accountant's role is that he usually stops short of taking the necessary action to achieve practical control. His task is to present information to management in such a form that action may be taken to correct deviations from plan. The principle of 'management by exception' means that only differences between planned and actual costs (variances) need to be spotlighted. If everything is running smoothly, there is no need to report in detail. Wherever possible, causes for the deviation will be indicated (variance analysis). The accountant's reports will therefore give as many clues as possible but, in the last analysis, it is management's job to put things right. In many cases it will be beyond the expertise of the accountant to suggest detailed remedies. Let us assume that the budget for a particular research project was fixed at £200,000. Already, £250,000 has been spent and no results are visible. The accountant can do little more than draw attention to the fact, and point out that if this happens frequently the business will soon be running at a loss. He has alerted management to a state of affairs that needs urgent investigation. What should they do? Write the project off, continue as planned, or modify the project? Perhaps the original £200,000 was unrealistic. The final decision will depend on technical as much as financial considerations.

The role of the management accountant varies between different organizations. In one company he may be merely a recorder of information, reporting variances, but powerless to do much about them. In another company he may be the effective controller, with power to initiate special investigations, and cooperating with management in deciding what action is necessary to correct variances. The practical contribution of the management accountant will depend on his status in the organization, his own personal qualities as a communicator and diplomat and the extent to which the company is cost conscious.

Corporate planning and long term financial management are different matters. At this level the business must be seen as a total system in which it is impossible to isolate finance from the marketing, technical and personnel aspects of the business. Let us imagine that the executive management board of Universal Holdings Limited is meeting to consider the suggestion that it should diversify into the widgets market. The marketing director has outlined the prospects, based on a market research study conducted by his staff. 'The new product would fit in well with our existing product range and we could market it through our existing channels of distribution.' There follows a far ranging discussion of all aspects of the proposal.

'How much would we need to spend on advertising to launch the product?' 'When would we start to get some benefit from this advertising expenditure?' 'What profit margins could we expect?' 'How is the widget market likely to develop over the next few years?' 'What are our competitors likely to do?' 'What are the pros and cons of building up our own production facility or taking over an existing widget manufacturer?' 'Should we make the whole widget ourselves or should we subcontract much of the work?' 'What would be the effect on total employment within the Group?' 'What would happen if the British economy failed to expand at the growth rates currently predicted?' 'Ought we to consider overseas markets?' 'How are we going to finance all this?' 'Is the return on the investment likely to be satisfactory?' The financial director takes a key part in these discussions. She was well prepared for the meeting because for the last month she had been testing the various options on the computer-based financial planning model. 'What is the financial effect of a decision to move into widgets?' Different assumptions about the initial cost of launching the product and the pattern of cash income in the years following would be tried out on the model to see the effect on future profit and loss accounts and balance sheets by following each course of action. 'What would happen to our cash flow if we doubled advertising expenditure in Year 1?'

If accountants are to act as financial advisers to businesses they need to know more than how to prepare a set of final accounts in accordance with the requirements of the Companies Act. The business accountant is a key member of the management team. There will always be a need for high-calibre accountants wherever difficult decisions are taken within complex organizations, large business corporations, non-profit making private organizations such as charities and public bodies such as government departments and local authorities. It is not therefore surprising that the accounting profession has traditionally been seen as one of the main routes to senior management positions.

4

The study of Accounting

Even the poor student studies and is taught only political economy, while the economy of living which is synonymous with philosophy is not even sincerely professed in our colleges. The consequence is, that while he is reading Adam Smith, Ricardo and Say, he runs his father in debt irretrievably.

Henry Thoreau, *Walden*

Professional studies

As we have already observed, accounting is a practical subject. A financial accountant setting up a system for controlling the debtors' accounts in the sales ledger or a management accountant installing a budgetary control system must understand the relevant accounting techniques and be able to set up practical systems for recording and classifying the basic data to meet the requirements of a particular organization. It is often said that 'learning by doing' is the only effective way of learning a practical subject and so professional bodies insist on a period of training often lasting several years before qualification to ensure that the trainee accountant has a wide experience of practical accounting work.

On the other hand it must be equally obvious that effective accountants must be familiar with a body of knowledge directly or indirectly affecting their work which must be learned by study 'off the job'. What is this basic body of knowledge which must be acquired by accountants if they are to reach a minimum standard of competence in the exercise of their profession? We shall attempt to answer this question in the first part of this chapter. Later we shall argue that modern accountants should have a much deeper understanding of the nature of the subject if they are to adapt to the rapid changes in accounting practice referred to in the previous chapter.

As a first step it is clear that our budding accountants must be familiar with the basic techniques of keeping a set of books. A distinction is often drawn between accounting and bookkeeping. Bookkeeping is usually described in terms of the routine task of collecting, recording and processing accounting data. Accounting is said to be concerned with the more creative aspects of the work such as installing and controlling the systems and presenting and interpreting results. In practice, however, it is difficult to draw a firm line between the two functions and the widespread use of computer-based information systems is making the distinction obsolete. In the world of computer technology routine data processing is now done on the computer and specialist systems analysts are employed to design computer-based information systems. It is more helpful to see accounting as a single continuous procession along the lines of the AAA definition mentioned earlier. Even if the professional accountant is more concerned with the final stages of the process of identification, measurement and communication, it is important that he understands the process as a whole. The value of an information system's output is dependent on the quality of the data which is fed into the system. Inaccurate, irrelevant or out-of-date basic data will turn the process into a management misinformation system. The old computer maxim puts it more tersely: 'garbage in – garbage out'.

In a business accounting information system, data are generated from many sources, usually in documentary form. Purchase orders, goods received notes, requisitions, despatch notes, invoices, the payroll and many other documents provide evidence of the innumerable transactions which make up the firm's activities. These source documents are collected and the details recorded in the appropriate account. This may be carried out by traditional methods of recording the entries manually in a set of books. Nowadays a computer is likely to be used to record, store and process the data, even in a relatively small firm. The information must be summarized, evaluated and communicated in an appropriate manner, usually in the form of accounting reports.

We have already noted that the modern accounting systems are still based on the principles of double entry bookkeeping as propounded by Pacioli. Although methods of recording and processing the data may change, the need to express the two-sided nature of a transaction in a logical manner remains as strong as ever. The accountant must understand the basic principles of the double entry system and be able to apply them to a whole range of situations from keeping the petty cash accounts to preparing a set of accounts for a multi-national corporation. When studying such accounting procedures, it is easy to make the mistake of trying to memorize a set of standard accounting entries by rote without understanding fully the economic processes which they represent. We have seen that accounting may be described as economic mapmaking or, if you prefer the mirror analogy, we might say that the accounting system should reflect the reality of the production process in financial terms. Once the economic nature of a business transaction has been thoroughly understood, the most appropriate method of recording the transaction in the accounts should be self-evident. No matter how complex or technical the transaction may be, the principle is the same. First understand the business reality behind the transaction and the accounting entries will be clear.

In addition to an understanding of accounting technique, accountants will need to be aware of the basic principles of finance. What are the main sources of short and long term finance available to his company or to his client? What are the procedures and practices of such institutions as banks, insurance companies and the stock market which they will encounter on a day-to-day basis? In more general terms we might say that accountants must be aware of the economic environment. A moment's thought will show that the mere collection of useful pieces of information about the different types of debentures, export procedures or the working of the money market will not be sufficient. Financial and economic institutions are interrelated and, to make any sense of the detail, accountants need to have some idea of how the total system works. They must therefore have some understanding of economic theory.

Finally, professional accountants must be familiar with the legal regulations and other external requirements if they are to give advice on such matters as taxation or company practice and be able to prepare a set of accounts in accordance with the latest SSAPs.

As many of these requirements are constantly changing the practising accountant must make a determined effort to keep up to date. Taxation is an obvious example. The regulations affecting income tax, corporation tax, value added tax, capital gains tax and all the other forms of taxation which plague businesses and/or individuals are modified each year in a Finance Act which gives effect to the Chancellor's Budget proposals. Changes are often introduced to plug gaps in the earlier regulations and it is perhaps inevitable that tax legislation is drafted in opaque legal language which tries to anticipate every possible move by a potential tax avoider. Accountants have a difficult time to keep up-to-date with tax changes in order to prepare accounts which will satisfy the Inland Revenue and give tax planning advice to their clients. It is not surprising that taxation work tends to be the province of specialists.

We have noted that it was difficult to make sense of financial and economic activities without some understanding of economic theory to give an overview of the detail. The same comment applies to legal knowledge. Before studying the detailed tax regulations, the accountant should be familiar with the structure and operation of the legal system and the significance of such basic legal concepts as contract, tort, crime and property. For instance, commercial law is essentially a development of the basic notion of contract through an examination of such special contracts as Sale of Goods, Hire Purchase contracts, agency and the relation between the banker and his customer. He must be aware, for instance, that the source of most taxation law is parliamentary legislation, whereas the rules of the law of contract have, in the main, evolved from precedents set by the courts when deciding actual disputes.

It is worth noticing in passing that the legal concept of contract is another aspect of the fundamental principle of duality which is inherent in both the concept of economic exchange and the technique of double-entry bookkeeping. In English law an unconditional offer must be matched by an unqualified acceptance before a valid contract is formed. It takes two sides to make a contract; any exchange involves at least two parties and an economic transaction must be recorded by two entries in the books.

So far we have been trying to assemble a sort of survival kit for professional accountants. In summary we have found that they require an understanding of accounting practice as applied to the business situations they are likely to encounter, general financial and economic knowledge, an understanding of the legal framework of accounting and a detailed knowledge of those external regulations and requirements which have a direct effect on their work. Nowadays accountants should also be familiar with modern information technology. At the very least they must know enough not to be overawed by computer specialists and ideally they should have acquired considerable 'hands on' experience of computer-based information systems.

We have, of course, been speaking in general terms. An accountant in industry will need to know more about management accounting techniques and an accountant in public practice will need to be fully conversant with auditing procedures. Other specialists, such as public service accountants, will need to understand public finance and so on.

It would be an undue exaggeration to say that until recently the syllabuses for the various professional accountancy bodies in the United Kingdom and Ireland were conceived in the way we have just described. It was felt that there was an essential stock of current knowledge which accountants must have before they were allowed to put up their brass plates or otherwise offer their services as qualified accountants. Nor should we belittle this concept as a valid objective. Accountants *do* need to know how to practice their trade, and they *do* need to be familiar with the relevant legislation. There is a lot to know and the professional examinations, particularly at the final stages, have always been a severe test of competence in the subject.

The difficulty with this approach to the study of accounting is that by itself it only prepares accountants for their current role. If it is true that accounting practice is changing rapidly, recently qualified accountants will have to develop their skills in many different directions during their careers. The best preparation for such an uncertain future is a deep understanding of the basic principles of the subject to supplement the practical application. Much of the detailed knowledge will become obsolete, but if the basic principles are thoroughly understood it becomes easier to apply them to new and possibly unforeseen circumstances. This is the explanation of the often quoted paradox that 'there is nothing so practical as a sound theory'. In recent times the professional associations have themselves accepted at least in part the logic of this situation. Examination questions are no longer merely tests of memory but are as likely to examine the candidate's ability to apply general principles to a particular problem.

The academic study of accounting

A more fundamental development has been the recognition of accounting as a separate academic discipline to be studied as a subject on a degree course. Although accounting has long been established in higher education in the United States, the subject is a relative newcomer in the British Isles. Although a small number of universities taught accounting before the 1939-45 war, it has only been in the last thirty years that the subject has taken off with degree courses in universities and polytechnics, research programmes in accounting topics and learned journals where current issues of theory and practice may be debated.

This expansion of accounting degree courses in the British Isles does not mean that accounting is a graduate profession in the same way as in the United States where the possession of a relevant accounting degree is the only route towards full professional status. As may be seen in Appendix B, professional bodies in the British Isles allow trainees to qualify through a variety of routes. Prior study of accounting on a degree course is encouraged by granting exemptions from the professional examinations but it is not a professional requirement.

This is not the place to enter into a detailed discussion of the advantages and disadvantages of our system. It may seem strange that, compared with such professions as medicine, the law and engineering, it is not considered essential for future accountants to study the fundamental principles of their subject in a coherent manner. We expect a doctor to have studied in some depth such basic disciplines as biology and chemistry as a necessary foundation for the clinical subjects. On the other hand, there may be a healthy pragmatism on the part of the professional accountancy bodies in wishing to guard jealously the standards of entry to the profession and reserving the right to recruit students from a variety of educational backgrounds. Whatever the merits of the case it is clear that an increasing number of registered student accountants are graduates and an increasing number of these have degrees in subjects which are relevant to accounting.

What should be the content of an academic course in accounting as compared with the skills and knowledge which would be required for the professional preparation of an accountant? Needless to say the graduate accountant will have acquired much of the basic accounting, legal and financial knowledge mentioned earlier, although at this stage he will not be familiar with some of the more detailed techniques and practices which are best learned during the accountant's professional training. Auditing is rarely taught in an accounting degree course, for example. The AAA definition is a useful starting point for our discussion of 'academic' accounting. It may be paraphrased by saying that accounting is concerned with the *measurement* and *communication* of information about *economic* activities. The three academic disciplines which look, in a fundamental way, at quantitative methods, economic activity and the concept of communication – mathematics, economics and behavioural science – are clearly at the root of the academic study of accounting. Because financial accounting practices need to be understood in a particular legal environment, the study of law is also of fundamental importance.

Mathematics Almost all the accounting methods we have introduced so far have required no more mathematical expertise than simple arithmetic. If, however, we move beyond recording transactions, balancing an account and presenting these balances in accounting reports towards the transformation and interpretation of this information, it is apparent that there is a whole armoury of mathematical techniques which could be used. Let us take the double entry system itself as an example. As an alternative to traditional accounts, it is possible to record the dual nature of each transaction within a simple matrix. Although the basic data is the same, this alternative method of presentation enables the powerful techniques of matrix algebra to be used in analysing the information. Complex quantitative relations must be expressed in correct mathematical form to avoid ambiguity and to enable equations to be solved and data interpreted.

Economics In his interpretive role the accountant may be able to choose from a number of statistical techniques to help in the assessment and presentation of accounting information. For instance, it is impossible for an auditor to test every single transaction for accuracy. The number of transactions selected for checking should be large enough to give a measure of confidence to the exercise and yet not too large for the cost of the audit to be prohibitive. Statistical sampling theory will help him to select the most efficient size of sample.

We have already noted the importance of a grounding in economic theory to the accountant. General theories of macroeconomics attempt to explain the basic relationships within an economy as a whole with a view to providing policy guidelines for governments. Businessmen need to be conscious of the main trends in the economic environment, as must the accountant as the recorder of economic events: inflation accounting is an obvious example. Another branch of economic theory examines the measuring of such interrelated concepts as value, income and capital which are of fundamental importance to the accountant. An understanding of economic theories of the firm is essential for the understanding of such matters of cost accounting technique as the analysis of cost behaviour, break-even analysis and pricing policy.

Behavioural science Accounting is a social science. Accountants communicate information to individual managers or clients or to groups such as the board or the shareholders of a company. The information usually relates to the working of a complex organization such as a business corporation, public utility or government agency. This description of the work of the accountant uses words such as 'groups', 'communication', 'information' and 'organization', emphasizing the point that accounting can only be understood in its social context. It is clear that accounting practitioners have much to learn from behavioural sciences such as sociology, social psychology and individual psychology, which examine human behaviour from their different perspectives.

For instance, an understanding of organizational structure and responsibilities is of fundamental importance in budgetary control. This management accounting technique is an attempt to co-ordinate all the operations of the business by expressing plans in financial terms. Budgets are related to the organization of the company, so that each manager's budget reflects his responsibilities. A system designed for a 'mechanistic' type of organization with precise, static, formal relationships would not work in a more fluid 'organic' type of organization. It is essential that managers should cooperate in the preparation of budgets, and agree that they set attainable goals. Production, sales and resource data on which budgets are based will come from the specialist departments. The accountant or budget officer will express these plans in financial terms. Co-ordination is often achieved through a budget committee consisting of senior managers, to make sure that budgets are compatible and realistic. Budgets are not mere paper exercises, but the means by which the company's policies are expressed, co-ordinated and controlled. Budgetary control can only be understood in terms of the organization's social and political processes.

Budgets are also used to control the performance of managers. The principle is that the actual results achieved by a manager will be compared with his predetermined budget and the difference between the two, or variance, is reported back to him as a guide for corrective action. It is, however, rather naïve to assume that as soon as an unfavourable variance is reported to a manager, he will try to put things right. Motivation is complex and too often accountants have concentrated on the setting of budgets and calculation of variances rather than the way in which the variance information is actually used by managers. The moral is not that budgets are a waste of time, if not positively harmful. It is rather that budgets relate to people and if the accountant sees them merely as exercises in arithmetic, he should not be surprised if things go wrong.

This discussion has taken us into the realm of 'behavioural accounting'. This study is in effect an interdiscipline drawing on social psychology and individual psychology as well as accounting practice. In fact the advanced study of accounting is always interdisciplinary. Contributions from economics, mathematics, behavioural science and accounting theory are welded together to provide fresh insights and guidance for accounting practice. Financial management, which explores such issues as working capital management, the capital structure of a company and dividend policy is one example of such a field of study. Management accounting is another interdiscipline and to conclude this rapid survey of the academic study of accounting we shall look briefly at one aspect of management accounting which draws heavily on economics and mathematics: accounting for managerial decisions.

Decision accounting The managers of a business must take decisions. What prices should be charged for the company's products? Should the company buy an expensive item of equipment? Is it cheaper to send a consignment by road or by rail? Should a new factory be opened and, if so, where? Should a component be manufactured by the company or bought outside? Some of these decisions are of major strategic importance, others are fairly routine operating decisions. In all cases, accurate, up-to-date accounting information, presented in a meaningful way, is the first step to rational decision taking.

Traditional accounting techniques may not give the best solution if the problem is complex. If management has a straight choice of sending a consignment by rail or by road, it is relatively easy to assess the financial implications of these two alternatives. If, on the other hand, the problem is to find the most efficient distribution system from a number of possibilities, it would be necessary to express the problem as a series of mathematical equations using the transportation model.

It is often possible to express complex business problems in mathematical terms. This approach is called Operational Research (OR) and a number of techniques with such delightful names as 'the Monte Carlo method', 'queuing theory', 'linear programming' and 'dynamic programming' have been developed to solve standard business problems. What is the optimum number of check-out points in a supermarket? What is the best mix of a range of products, each with a different profit margin and production constraints? When it is possible to express the problem in the form of a standard OR model, a computer 'package' may be used to perform the routine calculations leading to the optimum solution.

These techniques can be applied to solve *short* term problems where uncertainty about the future is not a major consideration. In the real world decisions are often taken which may have repercussions many years hence. Building a new factory or investing in expensive capital equipment involves a high initial cost which is unlikely to be justified unless we take into account the expected benefits from that investment over a number of years. How can accountants help to provide advice which will enable wise choices to be made?

The only satisfactory method of giving due allowance for the time element in these long run decisions uses the concept of discounting. The principle is quite simple. A pound today is worth more to me than a pound to be paid in one year's time. The preference for present cash rather than future cash can be expressed as a rate of discount. For instance, if a 10 per cent rate of discount is assumed, £10 to be paid in one year's time has the equivalent value of £9.09 paid today, and £10 to be paid in two years' time is the equivalent of £8.26 today. Another way of expressing the same relationship is to say that the present value of £10 in two years' time is £8.26, given a discount rate of 10 per cent.

Let us assume that a company wishes to evaluate a major capital project such as a proposal to install a computer-based manufacturing system in an engineering works. The first stage would be to estimate future net cash flows (income less expenditure) associated with this project over its estimated life. These net cash flows would then be discounted using the appropriate rate to arrive at the net present value of the proposed investment. In a time of relatively high interest rates, the time pattern of future cash flows is of crucial importance. By using discounted cash flow techniques, it is possible to give due weighting to the time factor when appraising capital projects. The problem of uncertainty about the future may be minimized, although not eliminated, by the application of probability theory to the calculations. We do not know for certain what will be the net cash income arising from the investment in, say, two years time. On the other hand the technical experts may be prepared to say that there is a 3 in 10 chance (0.3 probability) that the net cash income in year two will be £25,000, a 0.2 probability that it will be £30,000, etc. It is now possible to weigh each of these projected future cash incomes by the probability of them occurring to arrive at an expected return for each year. Without going into the detailed calculations, it should be apparent that by combining discounting techniques with probability theory, it should be possible for accountants to give due weighting to both future cash flow patterns and uncertainties when evaluating major projects. Modern technology is capital intensive. Business success depends to an increasing extent on skill and judgement in evaluating such high-cost projects. These proposals will originate with research scientists, engineers and other technical experts. The accountant's contribution is to prepare information about alternative proposals, so that any decision taken will at least be financially sound.

Developments in accounting

Our survey of the history of accounting in Chapter 1 showed how accounting practice has responded to economic, technological, social and political changes. Part of the fascination of accounting as a subject is to study these interactions – accounting never stays still. The high rates of inflation experienced in the 1970s, for instance, led to growing interest in inflation accounting amongst professional and academic accountants in the United Kingdom. As rates of inflation tended to be lower in the 1980s, the various alternative methods of accounting for changes in price levels were no longer the main subject of accounting debate. We shall therefore conclude this survey of accounting by outlining, however tentatively, the direction in which the subject is moving. Many of the key developments have been mentioned in passing but it may be helpful to bring together the main factors currently affecting accounting practice at least in the western capitalist world.

So far as economic influences are concerned, perhaps the most important single factor is the increasing size and complexity of business organization. There will always be a place for the small business firm and there is some evidence to suggest that in certain areas of high technology there is increasing scope for small businesses run by scientist/entrepreneurs. With this qualification, however, it is clear that most of the significant developments in accounting technique in recent years have been responses to the management and information problems caused by the growth of large multi-product and often multi-national corporations. Apart from the problems of co-ordination and control caused by the sheer size of the organization, increasing uncertainties in the business environment make long term planning difficult, particularly when many major capital projects have a lead time which may be measured in decades rather than years. Budgetary control, the measurement of divisional performance, group accounting and methods of appraising large capital projects are a few examples of areas of accounting practice which are responding to these challenges.

The impact of information technology on accounting practice has already been noted. It is now possible to process masses of data by computer more cheaply and quickly than by old clerical methods. These developments have three main effects on the work of the accountant. In the first place they reduce dramatically the time taken to present routine accounting information to managers. Prompt information is essential if effective corrective action is to be taken. Secondly the computer makes it possible to analyse information in a variety of ways to suit managerial needs. For instance, provided the data has been suitably coded, it is possible to analyse the month's sales by region, product, salesman, type of customer or in any other form as required with the minimum of effort. Finally the development of special software packages means that the accountant now has relatively easy access to such powerful analytical tools as statistical analysis, operations research and financial modelling. The use of such techniques should improve the accountant's ability to solve complex problems and make recommendations based on an analysis of alternative courses of action.

In spite of these considerable economic and technological changes, it could be argued that, in the long term, social and political changes will have the most important impact on the work of the accountant. There is an insatiable demand for more information about economic affairs and the advent of advanced information technology now makes it possible to supply these needs, at least in theory. For instance, there are continual demands for greater accountability from government departments and agencies. The free flow of information about all government actions which are not affected by security considerations is essential in a healthy democracy. Is the government using the taxpayers' money wisely? Such information as is available is often not easily accessible and difficult to understand, even by MPs. These comments apply with equal force to local government. The Report of the 1976 Committee of Enquiry into Local Government Finance[1] stated that 'Accountability to the electorate is the essence of local democracy. . . . For local accountability to be effective, however. . . the local electorate must be able to understand the financial facts about decisions taken by the local authority'.

How can the general public make informed judgements when information is so ill presented? Is it merely wishful thinking to suggest that there may perhaps be a role here for the skills of the accountant in his capacity as *communicator* of economic information?

At the moment, business accounting practice is to a large extent geared to the needs of shareholders and managers. However, all employees have a right to be well informed about the future prospects of the organization for which they work and this right is becoming more widely recognized. Collective bargaining might be more realistic and less acrimonious if the trade unions had some of the management accounting information available to the employers. Perhaps in the future published accounts will give information about the workforce, training and employment practices and other social matters. The French law of 1977 requiring certain companies to produce Social Balance Sheets (Bilans Socials) might point the way to further developments in social accounting. Under this law most companies have to give information (the amount of detail is dependent on the size of company) on such matters as numbers employed, dismissed and promoted; absenteeism; a detailed analysis of remuneration and fringe benefits; health and safety at work information; an analysis of training costs; working conditions, including length of the working week; information about expenditure on improvements in working

[1] Command paper 6453 (London, HMSO, 1976) p. 102.

conditions; information about trade union representation and joint consultative procedures, etc.

Of course, such statements are not financial accounting reports as normally understood. However, as the information needs expand, some of the traditional conventions about what types of information should be included in published accounts will begin to be questioned. How could it be said that the normal financial balance sheet gives a true and fair view of a high technology people business, such as a software house? Such a business does not need expensive buildings or equipment. The only assets of importance are the skill and expertise of the staff – unrecorded in the financial balance sheet.

This has been a rapid 'Cook's Tour' of accountancy covering current professional practice, the academic study of accounting and possible future developments in the subject. It is hoped that this picture of the role of accounting in the modern world may have dispelled any lingering image in the mind of the reader of the accountant as a Dickensian figure sitting on a high stool and poring over musty ledgers. Accounting is making an important contribution to the information revolution of the late twentieth century and the social consequences of these changes are likely to be no less dramatic than those following the Industrial Revolution of the late eighteenth century.

Appendix A: For further reading

This list is limited to books published in the United Kingdom. A number of excellent books published in the USA are also available. The latest edition is shown in each case.

Introductions for non-specialist readers
J. Sizer *An insight into Management Accounting* (Penguin, 2nd edn 1979)
R.H. Parker *Understanding Company Financial Statements* (Penguin, 2nd edn 1982)
A.P. Robson *Essential Accounting for Managers* (Cassell, 4th edn 1979)
G. Mott *Accounting for Non-Accountants* (Pan 1984)

Introductory texts intended for first year higher education courses in accounting
C. Nobes *Introduction to Financial Accounting* (George Allen and Unwin, revised edn 1983)
G.A. Lee *Modern Financial Accounting* (Nelson, 3rd edn 1981)
A. Hindmarch, M. Atchison and R. Marke *Accounting : An Introduction* (Macmillan 1977)
M.W.E. Glautier and B. Underdown *Accounting Theory and Practice* (Pitman, 2nd edn 1982)
R.J. Bull *Accounting in Business* (Butterworth, 4th edn 1980)
F.P. Langley *Introduction to Accounting for Business Studies* (Butterworth, 4th edn 1978)

Specialist topics and recent developments

B. Carsberg and T. Hope (eds) *Current Issues in Accounting* (Philip Allan, 2nd edn 1984)
A. Hopwood and C. Tompkins (eds) *Issues in Public Sector Accounting* (Philip Allan 1984)

C.W. Nobes and R.H. Parker (eds) *Comparative International Accounting* (Philip Allan 1981)

J. Arnold, B. Carsberg and R Scapens (eds) *Topics in Management Accounting* (Philip Allan 1980)

A. Hopwood *Accounting and Human Behaviour* (Accounting Age Books 1974)

B.A. Rutherford *Financial Reporting in the Public Sector* (Butterworth 1983)

J. Arnold and T. Hope *Accounting for Management Decisions* (Prentice-Hall International 1983)

M. Bromwich and A.G. Hopwood *Essays in British Accounting Research* (Pitman 1981)

A.C. Littleton and B.S. Yamey *Studies in the History of Accounting* (Sweet and Maxwell 1956)

M. Bromwich *Economics of Capital Budgeting* (Penguin 1976)

T.A. Lee *Company Financial Reporting* (Van Nostrand Reinhold (UK), 2nd edn 1982)

Careers in Accounting

B.T. Houlden *Degree Course Guide: Business, Management and Accountancy* (Careers Research and Advisory Service (CRAC), Hobsons Press (Cambridge) Ltd, yearly editions)

DOG (Directory of Opportunities for Graduates) *Guide to Accountancy and Finance* (VNU Business Publications, yearly editions)

C. Nobes *Becoming an Accountant* (Longman 1983)

Appendix B: Undergraduate courses in Accounting in the United Kingdom

Each year the Accounting Education Consultative Board publishes a list of approved courses for accountancy education. Apart from full time Accountancy Foundation Courses and Graduate Conversion Courses, most courses listed are undergraduate courses at British universities, polytechnics and colleges. All these courses are recognized as leading to full exemption from the foundation stages of the examinations of the major accountancy bodies (ICAEW, ACA, ICMA, CIPFA). Limited exemptions from the professional stage examinations of certain bodies may also be possible. However, as the following short selection from this long list shows, not all approved accounting degree courses are necessarily labelled 'accounting' or 'accountancy'.

Institution	Title of approved degree
Aberdeen University	MA(Ord) Accountancy
University of Aston in Birmingham	BSc Managerial and Administrative Studies
Bath University	BSc Business Administration
Belfast, the Queens University	BSc (Economics)
	BSSc Major in Business
City of Birmingham Polytechnic	BA Accountancy
University of Birmingham	BCom Accounting
Bradford University	BSc Business Studies
Brighton Polytechnic	BA Accounting and Finance
	BA(Hons) Business Studies
Bristol University	BSc in Social Sciences, Economics and Accounting

etc.

Such 'relevant' degrees must each contain elements of accounting, quantitative subjects, economics and law to secure recognition by the Board. In some cases (Economics degrees, for example) approval depends on the successful completion of certain accounting options within the course. However, there is considerable variation within this basic framework: some courses emphasize 'professional' aspects, in other cases accounting is studied within the context of a more general business studies or social sciences degree. It is possible to link accounting studies with economics, computing, languages, law, management science, statistics and mathematics. The prospective student has a wide choice!

The following example may serve to illustrate the basic curriculum of a 'typical' accounting degree.

Trent Polytechnic: BA Accounting and Finance

Year 1	Accounting; Accounting information processing; Economics; Law; Introduction to behavioural studies; Quantitative methods
Year 2	Financial accounting; Managerial accounting and finance; Accounting information processing; Commercial law; Organizational studies; Quantitative methods
Year 3	Placement year and project
Year 4	Core subjects: Financial accounting; Managerial accounting and finance; Organizational decision making; Options (two to be chosen): Accounting and finance in the public sector; International finance; Insurance principles and practice; Company law; Operational research; Computing and accounting; Comparative accounting systems

Note that this is an example of a four-year sandwich degree where the third year is spent gaining practical experience in industry, a practising office or public service accounting. Most 'relevant' degrees in England and Wales are three-year full-time courses. More detailed information about the various courses may be obtained from university or college prospectuses and course booklets. The University Central Council on Admissions (UCCA) handbook is also useful. The Careers Research and Advisory Centre (CRAC) publishes a useful analysis of all business and accounting courses currently available, with comparative information about the balance and content of courses, selection procedures and staffing (see list of further reading). It is unusual for specific 'A' level subjects to be required for admission to an accounting degree course, although, other things being equal, some preference may be given to students studying such subjects as mathematics and economics at 'A' level. Good evidence of numeracy and literacy at 'O' level or its equivalent is always required. A final word of warning: Accounting is becoming a popular, over subscribed subject and it means that each year prospective students are asked to achieve higher 'A' level grades than the previous year. It is impossible to be specific about the grades likely to be set in the offer of a place at university or polytechnic. Some undergraduate courses are more popular than others and admission policies vary between institutions. However, a student who has low 'A' level grades in two subjects is unlikely to be successful in obtaining a place on an accounting degree course. The more popular courses, with a limited number of available places, may require three high 'A' level grades for admission.

Some more general guides to higher education include *The student book* published annually by Macmillan (Papermac); P. Wilby, *The Sunday Times good university guide* (Granada); B. Heap, *Complete degree course offers: winning your place at university, polytechnics and other institutions of higher education* (Careers Consultants); J.K. Gilbert (ed), *Staying the course: how to survive higher education* (Kogan Page, 1984); and *Higher education in the United Kingdom* (Longman).

What are the career prospects for accounting graduates? Tables B1 and B2 give some indication of the recent position, although there are undoubtedly more opportunities in industry and the public service than Table B2 suggests.

Table B1: First known destinations of first degree students 1979–81 (polytechnic and university graduates combined)

	Accounting graduates	Graduates in all subjects
	%	%
Permanent home employment	90.5	54.1
Permanent overseas employment	0.4	2.3
Research or academic study	1.4	11.2
Teacher training	0.5	9.0
Other training (e.g. social work, law)	1.3	8.8
Employment short term	1.9	5.2
Unemployed at 31 December following graduation	4.0	9.4
	100.0	100.0
Total numbers of graduates	3171	211228

Source: Bourner, T. *Graduates' first destinations*, Council for National Academic Awards, 1984

Table B2: Employment categories of the 2,837 first degree graduates who gained UK home employment for 1979–81 (polytechnic and university graduates combined)

	%
Public service	2.7
Education	0.5
Manufacturing industries	9.0
Other industries (including building, public	1.6
utilities, transport) accountancy firms	78.2
Banking and insurance	4.5
Other commerce	2.4
Other UK home employment	1.1
	100.0

Appendix C: Becoming an accountant

This book is not intended as a complete careers guide to the accounting profession. As the reader of Chapter 3 will have gathered, the subject is complicated by the fact that there are six separate professional bodies in the British Isles, each with their own education and training regulations. The following outline sets out the main choices which must be made by anyone contemplating a career in accountancy. Professor Nobes' short book *Becoming an Accountant* gives more detail about these matters, but as regulations are always subject to revision the serious enquirer must consult the appropriate professional bodies direct to find out the up-to-date position.

1. Should I become a *professional* accountant?
It is possible to have a worthwhile career in accounting without necessarily obtaining full professional status. Accounting technicians may take the AAT qualification or an appropriate BTEC course. At the same time many graduates do not become professionally qualified accountants but see their degree as a base for a career in general business or finance.

2. Which accounting *specialism* should I follow?
Chapter 3 describes the main accounting specialisms: public practice, management accounting and public service accounting, and introduces the reader to the six professional accounting bodies recognized in the British Isles. Remember that only members of the three Chartered Institutes and certain certified accountants may hold practising certificates. Although the ICMA is the specialist management accounting body, many members of the other professional bodies hold positions as management accountants in industry, commerce and public service organizations. Similarly, public service accounting is not the sole prerogative of CIPFA members. An ICAEW member may therefore start his or her career in practice but move into management accounting or the public service later on. Before making this choice of institute or accounting specialism it is important to read *all*

the relevant literature and, if possible, discuss the issues with accountants working in the different specialisms.

Table C1 shows the growth in the membership of the four England and Wales based professional bodies over the period 1965 to 1983. Accountants resident outside Britain are included (a significant proportion of ACA and ICMA members). The figures clearly indicate that there has been a steady increase in the demand for the services of all types of qualified accountants over this period.

Table C1: Growth in membership of four professional accountancy bodies

	ACA	CIPFA	ICMA	ICAEW
1965	11476	4063	9200	40759
1970	12963	5349	11436	49725
1975	16045	7224	14969	61718
1980	22732	8620	19285	71677
1983	26052	8983	22164	78231

3 What route should I take towards qualification?

In addition to satisfying the training and experience requirements of the chosen professional body a registered accounting student should also follow an approved educational route towards final professional qualification.

Professional bodies draw a distinction between foundation stage examinations and professional examinations. Although most professional bodies set their own foundation stage examinations, it is usual for students to obtain exemption from this stage through successful completion of an approved higher education course. This might be an approved, relevant degree course in accounting (see next section), or a one year full time foundation course in accounting at a polytechnic or college. Holders of partially relevant degrees in such subjects as economics, law, or mathematics may also obtain exemptions from individual subjects in the foundation stage examinations. (The ICMA may give full exemption from the foundation stage to such graduates.)

The professional bodies also encourage graduates in other disciplines – the natural sciences and humanities for instance – to enter the accounting profession. The ICAEW and CIPFA allow such graduates to follow an intensive graduate conversion course which gives foundation stage exemptions. The ICMA and the ACA give certain exemptions to such graduates even though they may not have followed an equivalent course of study in their degree.

The prospective student has therefore the choice of a number of different educational routes towards qualification. These paths converge at the professional examination stages. The professional bodies prefer to set these examinations themselves, although the ICMA, ACA and CIPFA may give certain limited professional status exemptions to relevant degree holders. The professional examinations have a reputation for difficulty; certainly the proportion of candidates passing at the first attempt is depressingly low for most of the professional bodies. Whichever route is chosen, the paths from 'A' levels to professional qualifications are long and arduous. Professional accounting students need ability, motivation *and* stamina.

Appendix D: Useful addresses

The Institute of Chartered Accountants in England and Wales
PO Box 433
Chartered Accountants' Hall
Moorgate Place
London EC2P 2BJ

enquiries also to:
399 Silbury Boulevard
Witan Gate East
Milton Keynes MK9 2HL

The Institute of Chartered Accountants of Scotland
27 Queen Street
Edinburgh EH2 1LA

The Association of Certified Accountants
(Incorporated by Royal Charter)
29 Lincoln's Inn Fields
London WC2 3EE

enquiries also to:
1 Woodside Place
Glasgow 93 7QF

The Institute of Cost and Management Accountants
(Incorporated by Royal Charter)
63 Portland Place
London W1N 4AB

The Chartered Institute of Public Finance and Accountancy
2–3 Robert Street
London WC2N 6BH

The Institute of Chartered Accountants in Ireland
7 Fitzwilliam Place
Dublin 2

The Institute of Chartered Accountants in Ireland
14 Donegal Square South
Belfast BT1 5JE

Accounting Education Consultative Board
11 Copthall Avenue
London EC2P 2BJ

Business and Technician Education Council (BTEC)
Central House
Upper Woburn Place
London WC1H 0HH

Association of Accounting Technicians
21 Jockey's Fields
London WC1R 4BN

Index

Index